NFT
FOR BEGINNERS

Making Money with Non-Fungible Tokens

Nathan Real

Table of Contents

INTRODUCTION

NATHAN REAL

Introduction

NFT is getting more popular because it is more economical and produces bigger profits, thus, stimulating the interest of the population. This book will teach you all you need to know about NFT and Crypto Art. NFTs are the abbreviation for non-fungible tokens, and an NFT is analogous to the playing card you've already collected as a child in the digital world. Video, artwork, audio, and even book all are possibilities in NFT technology. It's just a virtual document containing ownership information saved on the Blockchain, and that's all there is to it. NFTs are currently thriving in various fields, and they will have a substantial impact on the creative world shortly.

If you're a writer, you should pay attention to how they should disrupt the industry. A digital commodity that may understand actual goods, including music, artwork, in-game items, and movies—NFTs are becoming more popular. However, even though they had been around since the early 2000s, NFTs are gradually becoming more popular as a method of making online artwork. Hackers may readily replicate vector illustrations on the web; but, if you utilize NFTs, you'll discover a way of preserving a track record of possession or authenticity that can be used to protect your intellectual property. Are you ready to make your first non-fungible token investment? Do you have the necessary funds?

When learning about the intricate realm of NFTs, the NFTs industry, and making more educated decisions in the virtual token business, this book will serve you as an excellent beginning point. In today's marketplace, there is a range of systems available to aid users in getting started with NFT trading. This book is meant

to offer you the knowledge and skills necessary to succeed in NFT trading, with the overall objective of securing the financial freedom of its readers. Most people your age isn't exposed to this kind of stuff, so proceed with caution. Please treat nature with respect and understand its value.

The essential thing to do is put it to appropriate use. It's incredibly potent, and if you put in the necessary work and time, it has the potential to revolutionize your life dramatically. Here's what you'll learn about making money as a non-traditional investor and why investing with them is a smart choice!

CHAPTER 1

WHAT ARE NFTS?

NATHAN REAL

Chapter 1.
WHAT ARE NFTS?

A non-fungible token, likewise termed NFT, is a type of data unit that is both unique and non-transferable, held on a blockchain, a kind of digital ledger. NFTs can be connected with digital items that can be reproduced, such as photographs, movies, and audio. NFTs use a digital ledger to give a certificate of authenticity/evidence of ownership. Still, they do not prohibit exchanging or duplicating the actual digital files stored on the computer. Because NFTs are not interchangeable (fungible), they differ from blockchain-based cryptocurrencies such as Bitcoin in this respect. When it comes to the energy costs and carbon footprint connected with confirming blockchain transactions, as well as their widespread usage in art frauds, NFTs have come under fire. Further concerns question the utility of producing evidence of ownership in a market that is frequently uncontrolled and beyond the legal system.

1.1 Reality of NFTs

Non-fungible tokens are cryptographic assets that exist on a blockchain and are distinguished from one another by having unique identifier codes and information. Unlike cryptocurrencies, they cannot be traded or swapped at face value. It is indifferent to fungible tokens, such as cryptocurrencies, which are all identical and may be used as a medium for economic transactions to be carried out. Bitcoin and other cryptocurrencies, like actual money, are fungible, which means that they may be traded or swapped for one another. For example, the value of a single Bitcoin is always the same as the value of another Bitcoin. Similarly, one Ethereum is always equivalent to another unit of Ether. Because of their fungibility, cryptocurrencies are well-suited for use as a safe means of exchange in the digital economy, where they have gained widespread acceptance.

Because each token is exclusive and irreplaceable, NFTs alter the cryptographic paradigm, making it nearly impossible for a non-fungible token to be considered the same as another. Tokens are digital representations of assets that have been compared to digital passports because each token carries a unique, non-transferable identity that allows it to be distinguished from the other tokens in circulation. They are also extendable, which means that you may combine two NFTs to create a third, one-of-a-kind NFT by breeding them together. NFTs, like Bitcoin, have ownership information that allows token holders to be easily identified and transferred between one another. In addition, NFTs enable asset owners to provide information or qualities relevant to the item. For instance, in the case of coffee beans, tokens representing the beans might be recognized as fair trade. Alternatively, artists may mark their digital artwork by including their mark in the information associated with it.

NFTs were developed because of the ERC-721 standard. ERC-721 is a smart contract standard set by some individuals liable for the ERC-20 smart contract standard. It defines the bare minimum interface required for swapping and allocating gaming tokens, including ownership details, safety, and metadata. The ERC-1155 bar lowers the transactional and storage costs associated with non-fungible tokens while batching various NFTs into a single contract. The CryptoKitties' use of NFTs is perhaps the most well-known. CryptoKitties, which were first announced in November 2017, are digital representations of kitties that have been assigned unique identifiers on Ethereum's distributed ledger. All the kittens are different and have their ether pricing. These creatures procreate amongst themselves and generate new offspring, each of whom has unique characteristics and values compared to their parents. Following its inception, CryptoKitties quickly gained a large following, with fans spending more than $20 million in Ether (Ethereum) to purchase, feed, and otherwise care for them in their first few weeks. It is estimated that some fans spent over $100,000 on the endeavor. Though the CryptoKitties' use case may seem inconsequential, the ones that follow it have far-reaching commercial ramifications. For example, non-fungible tokens (NFTs) have been employed in private equity and real estate transactions. Incorporating numerous sorts of tokens into a single contract has many ramifications, one of which being the capacity to serve as an escrow for various forms of NFTs, ranging from art to real estate, all inside the same financial transaction.

Each NFT has a unique structure that can be used in various applications. Examples include the digital representation of tangible assets such as real estate and artwork, particularly well-suited. The fact that they are built on blockchains means that they may also be used to eliminate middlemen, link artists with audiences, or even manage user identities. NFTs can eliminate intermediaries, simplify transactions, and open up new markets.

In the present market for NFTs, collectibles such as digital artworks, sports cards, and rare items account for a significant market share. The most talked-about location is probably NBA Top Shot, where you can collect NBA NFTs in the form of digital cards. Several of these cards had fetched millions of dollars when they were auctioned. "Just setting up my Twitter," wrote Jack Dorsey in the first tweet ever written, which he sent over Twitter.

The NFT of the world's first tweet has already fetched up to $2.5 million in bidding.

An NFT is just a unit of data recorded on a digital ledger known as a blockchain and maybe sold and exchanged in the cryptocurrency world. When an NFT is linked with a specific physical or digital asset, the asset may be used for a particular purpose, and the NFT can be used to grant permission to use the property for that purpose. An NFT (and the related license to use copy) can be purchased and sold in the digital marketplace. In most cases, the extralegal character of NFT trading leads to an unofficial transfer of ownership over an item that has no legal foundation for implementation and which frequently confers little more than the ability to act as a social status symbol.

NFTs perform the same functions as cryptographic tokens. Non-transferable tokens (NFTs) are formed when blockchains string tracks of cryptographic hash, a collection of characters specifying a collection of data, over previous records, resulting in a chain of recognizable data blocks. Because each digital file is authenticated via a digital signature, this cryptographic transaction procedure may be used to trace who owns which NFTs. On the other hand, data linkages that refer to specifics such as where the artwork is kept may become invalidated.

1.2 Importance of NFTs

Compared to the relatively basic notion of cryptocurrencies, non-fungible tokens represent a significant advancement. Modern finance systems are contained of complex trading and financing systems for a wide range of asset kinds, spanning from property investment to loan contracts to artwork, among other things. NFTs provide a huge step forward in reconstructing this infrastructure by creating virtual representations of physical assets.

The digital representation of real assets and unique identifiers are not new concepts. Nevertheless, when these ideals are joined with the advantages of a tamper-resistant blockchain of smart contracts, they become a powerful force for positive change. The efficiency of the market is perhaps the most evident advantage of NFTs. A physical item converted into a digital asset accelerates operations and eliminates mediators. The use of non-fungible tokens (NFTs) to represent digital or physical art on a blockchain removes the need for agents and enables artists to communicate with their audiences directly. They may also help to increase the efficiency of company procedures. It will be simpler for various players in the supply chain to engage with an NFT for a wine bottle, and it will aid in tracking the bottle's origin, manufacturing, and sale throughout the whole process. One of Ernst & Young's customers has already benefited from such a solution designed by the consulting company. NFTs are also suitable for use in the context of identity management. Consider the example of real passports, which must be shown at every entrance and departure point. When individuals' tokens are converted into National Identification Cards, it becomes possible to simplify the access and leave procedures for jurisdictions worldwide within each unique identifying quality. Furthermore, NFTs may be utilized for identity management in the digital environment, extending the previous use case.

In addition, non-fungible tokens (NFTs) may democratize investment by fractionalizing tangible assets such as real estate. It is simpler to split a virtual real estate asset between numerous owners than to divide a physical real estate asset among many owners. This tokenization principle does not have to be limited to real estate it can be applied to other purchases. As a result, artwork does not necessarily have to be owned by a single individual. Multiple people may hold the artwork's digital version, each accountable for a different portion of the painting. Such partnerships have the potential to increase the company's value and income. The establishment of new marketplaces and types of investment represents the most intriguing prospect for non-fungible tokens. Think of a chunk of land that has been subdivided into many segments, each of which comprises a distinct set of features and various sorts of property. One of the parts may be located near a beach, another is an entertainment venue, and another is a residential neighborhood. An NFT represents a unique chunk of land, and each piece of land is valued differently based on its unique attributes. It is possible to make real estate dealing, which is a complicated and bureaucratic endeavor, more straightforward by adding important information into each NFT.

The blockchain-based virtual reality platform Decentraland, which runs on Ethereum's network, has already implemented this notion. As non-fungible tokens (NFTs) grow more advanced and are connected to the finance system, it may become feasible to apply the same idea of tokenized parcels of land, each with various values and locations, in the real world.

1.3 Plagiarism in NFTs

There have been instances when "artists' work" has been duplicated without their consent and marketed as a non-fungible token. The designer Qing Han departed in 2020, and a scammer used her identity to sell a bunch of her paintings as non-fungible tokens (NFTs) after she was discovered to be deceased. In a similar vein, a seller portraying as Banksy sold an NFT created by the designer for $336,000 in 2021, but the seller in the given instance reimbursed the money when the matter received widespread media notice.

It is also thinkable for a scammer to mint an NFT inside an artist's wallet and then transfer it to their wallet without the artist's knowledge using a practice known as "sleepminting." It is provided an opportunity for hackers to create a bogus NFT that seemed to have come from the wallet of an American artist known as Beeple. According to the BBC, on the NFT marketplace, OpenSea, employees engaged in insider trading when they purchased NFTs before being introduced. They understood what they would be advertised on their main website before launching. NFT buying and selling is an unregulated industry with no legal repercussions for those who engage in such misconduct.

Adobe suggested the creation of a database for the cosmos, File System, as an alternate method of confirming the validity of digital works when they announced the development of NFT compatibility for the graphic editor Photoshop in their release of NFT support for Photoshop.

Owning an NFT does not automatically confer intellectual property rights on the digital asset that the token represents, as is often believed. Even though somebody might sell an NFT reflecting their work, the new buyer will not automatically obtain copyright protections when custody of the NFT is transferred. As a result, the original owner will be permitted to generate more NFTs representing the same work. An NFT is just evidence of possession that is distinct from copyright protection. Rebecca Tushnet, a law researcher, claims that "in a sense, the purchaser obtains whichever the art world believes they have received when they make the purchase. Unless the copyright to the actual work is expressly transferred, they do not in any way own the rights to it." However, customers of NFTs do not often obtain ownership of the original artwork.

CHAPTER 2

HISTORY OF NFT

NATHAN REAL

Chapter 2.
HISTORY OF NFT

Quantum, the first known NFT, was produced by Kevin McCoy & Anil Dash in May 2014 and consisted of a video clip generated by McCoy's wife Jennifer and other components. During a live session for Seven-on-Seven conferences at the New Museum of New York, McCoy entered the footage on the Namecoin network and sold it to Dash for $4 on the Namecoin network. As McCoy and Dash put it, the technique was referred to as "monetized graphics." A non-fungible, which was expressly tied to a one-of-a-kind piece of art (enabled by Namecoin). Compared to the multiple-unit, exchangeable "colored coins" of those other blockchains, including Counterparty, are not fungible and do not include metadata.

Three calendar months after making the Ethereum blockchain, the very first NFT venture, Etheria, was announced and exhibited at DEVCON 1, Ethereum's inaugural developer conference, in London, United Kingdom, in October 2015. After not getting sold for more than five years, most of Etheria's 457 tradable hexagonal tiles were finally snapped up on 13 March 2021, when revived interest in NFTs ignited a purchasing frenzy. For a total of $1.4 million, all tiles were sold in less than 24 hours.

The release of the ERC-721 standard initially suggested on the Ethereum GitHub in 2017 was followed by the launch of several NFT initiatives that year. The word NFT received widespread acceptance. Curio Cards, CryptoPunks (a project to trade one-of-a-kind cartoon characters, developed by the American company Larva Labs and distributed on the Ethereum blockchain), and the Decentraland platform are examples of such projects. All three initiatives were mentioned in the initial proposal, and a set of unique Pepe trading cards were included.

The popularity of CryptoKitties, a blockchain game in which participants adopt and exchange virtual kittens, sparked public interest in non-fungible tokens. Soon after its introduction, the idea went viral, generating $12.5 million and resulting in the sale of certain kittens for more than $100,000 per kitty. The popularity of CryptoKitties led to the addition of CryptoKitties to the ERC-721 standards, which was formed in January 2018 (and completed in June). It confirmed the usage of the phrase "non-fungible token" to refer to NFT.

In 2018, Decentraland, a virtual world based on blockchain that launched its token sales in August 2017, $20 million was the size of its internal market. As of September 2018, $26 million were raised in an "ico" (initial coin offering) and had a total market capitalization of $26 million.

Following the success of CryptoKitties, another comparable NFT-based online game, Axie Infinity, was created in March 2018 and ended up becoming the most expensive NFT collection in May 2021, after which it was discontinued.

In 2019, Nike received a patent for a system known as Crypto-Kicks, which would employ NFTs to check the integrity of actual shoes and provide the consumer with a virtual replica of the shoe in exchange for their payment.

During the first quarter of 2020, Dapper Labs, the company that created CryptoKitties, unveiled the preview version of NBA Top Shot, a project that would offer tokenized memorabilia of NBA highlights.

The project was created on top of the Flow blockchain, a younger and more powerful blockchain than the Ethereum blockchain.

Later that year, the program was made available to the public, and as of 28 February 2021, it has generated over $230 million in total revenues.

During 2020, the NFT market enjoyed fast expansion, with its total value doubling to $250 million. NFTs accounted for more than $200 million in spending during the first three months of 2021.

Following a series of high-profile transactions, interest in non-fungible tokens (NFTs) rose in the first few months of 2021. Digital art made by the artist Grimes, the NFT of a Nyan Cat meme, and NFTs designed by 3LAU to advertise his album *Ultraviolet* were among the NFTs sold in February 2021. NFT sales were made in more publicized ways in March 2021, including an NFT created to market the Kings of Leon album *When You See Yourself*, a $69.3 million sale of digital work by Mike Winkelmann titled *Everydays: the First 5000 Days*, and an NFT created by the founder of Twitter Jack Dorsey that represented his first tweet. Because of the nature of the NFT market, more investors are trading at higher volumes and rates. Experts have referred to the recent spike in NFT purchases as an economic bubble and have likened this to the Dot-com boom. By the middle of April 2021, demand looked to have significantly waned, resulting in a dramatic drop in prices; early purchasers were said to have "done extraordinarily well" by the publication Bloomberg Businessweek. Sotheby's in London auctioned off an NFT of the source code for the World Wide Web, which was ascribed to internet creator computer scientist Professor Tim Berners-Lee in June 2021, and the piece went for US$5.4 million.

According to the auction house, Sotheby's auctioned around 101 NFTs (Bored Ape Yacht Club) worth $24.4 million in September 2021. ETH393 ($1.3 million) was paid for a complete set of Curio Cards, including the "17b" mistake on 1 October 2021, marking the first time that lives to bid at an auction was handled in Ether. A CryptoPunk, other cat-based NFTs, and a Pepenopoulos, rare Pepe, 2016, were sold for a combined total of $3.6 million at a Sotheby's auction later that month. In addition, this was the first auction presented on Sotheby's "Metaverse," a platform devoted particularly to NFT collectors, and it is planned to become a biennial event.

During the 27 March 2021 Saturday Night Live episode, characters explained non-fungible tokens (NFTs) to Treasury Secretary of US Janet Yellen, who Kate McKinnon portrayed.

A grown-up version of Butters Stotch in his Dr. Chaos avatar tricked people into buying NFTs in the Paramount+ TV film *South Park: Post Covid: The Return of Covid*, which aired on Cartoon Network in 2013. Even though they are shown as a bad investment in the film, he has become so skilled at selling them that he has been sent to a mental facility.

2.1 First NFT

So, what is the root of this technological craze? NFTs and the man who designed them, Kevin McCoy, have a storied history that began on 3 May 2014. Quantum, a non-fungible currency, was established by him long before the crypto art business took off.

Quantum appears to be a pixelated design of an octagon crammed with forms that all share the same center, with more oversized shapes enclosing smaller firms and fascinating pulsating in dazzling hues, as shown on the Quantum website. It is now on the market for $7 million as part of only one "Quantum" art project (2014–2021).

McCoy is a one-of-a-kind figure in the Star Trek universe. Throughout the years, he and his girlfriend Jennifer have established themselves as the best digital painters in the industry. In McCoy's opinion, "the NFT phenomenon is deeply established in the art business." "It evolved out of a long custom of artists trying out new technology," says the author. As McCoy has done, the artist prefers to sell their work via galleries or one-on-one rather than participating in public pricing battles. The exhibit *Every Episode, Every Shot* is presently on display at the Art Museum.

Artists, entrepreneurs, businesses, writers and filmmakers, social media superstars, and even everyday people may create an NFT by collaborating. There is no need for previous expertise, and anyone may mint an NFT as far as they can demonstrate that they generated or legally held the material in question. To get started using Portion, follow our step-by-step instructions on designing an NFT.

CryptoPunks & CryptoKitties are only a few cultural trends that inspired the CryptoArt genre. Due to extensive network effects and the desire to pay considerable amounts of money to acquire them, these pieces of "art" became renowned.

2012–2013

Let's start this journey including various people, artists, and organizations. A "colored coin influenced NFTs," initially launched on the Bitcoin blockchain in 2012–2013 and has since gained widespread acceptance. Colored coins are blockchain technology tokens that represent real-world assets. They may be used to prove ownership of a wide range of assets, including metals, autos, real industrial property, stocks, and bonds, among other things. The initial idea was to use the Bitcoin network to store digital artifacts such as coupons, real estate, corporate shares, and different types of information. They were regarded as cutting-edge technology with the significant unmet possibility of future applications in several fields.

2014

A mentorship banking platform with a distributed, open-web protocol based on the Bitcoin blockchain was built in 2014 by R. Dermody and E. Wagner as part of the Bitcoin blockchain community. Counterparty created a framework for anyone to develop their transferrable currencies/coins by allowing for asset creation and decentralized exchange, which enabled them to do so. It had a plethora of excellent ideas and opportunities, particularly in meme trading without the issues associated with counterfeiting.

2015

Counterparty formed a collaboration with the Spells of Genesis creators in April 2015. Using Counterparty, the developers of the videogame Spells of Genesis were not only among the first to put in-game assets into a blockchain, but they were also among the first to make an initial coin offering (ICO). The creators of Counterparty were able to contribute to the game's development by creating their in-game currency, BitCrystals.

2017

The characters developed by J. Watkinson & M. Hall, the inventors of Larva Labs, are one-of-a-kind. In recent years, rare Pepe's trade has gained popularity on the Ethereum platform. There'd be no two characters that were the same, and the total number of characters would be limited to 10,000 characters in total. The term CryptoPunks relates to a Bitcoin experiment from the 1990s, and the project may be thought of as a hybrid of the ERC721 and ERC20 protocols.

CryptoKitties NFTs were created with the help of the ERC721 protocol. They are a digital game based on the Ethereum network that allows players to adopt, foster, and trade virtual cats with other players across the world. They were incredibly well-known, and their appearances on major news sites such as CNBC & Fox News were well-publicized. Axiom Zen, a Vancouver-based company, created CryptoKitties, and it quickly gained popularity, garnering money from famous investors due to its fast expansion. When Axiom Zen acquired CryptoKitties, Dapper Labs was renamed to distinguish it from the original company.

2018–2021

NFTs progressively acquire public attention between 2018 and 2021 before exploding into widespread usage in the first half of 2021.

The allegedly secret movement that has swept the crypto realm has gradually grown into a more widely recognized kind of art and culture.

The non-fungible tokens services business is more efficient and liquid than conventional asset-transfer strategies. Several internet platforms have sprung up, each with its features for both manufacturers and collectors. The most significant area of disruption is focused on reducing centralized fees, which can be as high as 40% for conventional art traders and auction houses. The OpenSea is the most critical market for art, music, souvenirs domain names, and trading cards globally. Mintable's platform is intended to make the minting process as easy as possible for authors, and it does so via the use of APIs. According to the section, an NFT system permits Defis, NFTs, and DAOs, with the society controlling the governing token, which is $PRT. The purchase of "shards," which are ERC20 tokens representing a piece of a full NFT, is also likely on other platforms, such as Nintex, which allows users to buy fractions of NFTs, sometimes known as "fractions of NFTs."

2.2 Metaverse: The Future

Numerous companies are now involved in the development of virtual reality metaverses. Metaverses are virtual environments where the internet is brought to life in its simplest form. You can create your own life, interact with real individuals in an online community, design your avatar, play, work, and explore new spaces by utilizing virtual reality headsets or virtual or augmented glasses, smartphone apps, or other devices that incorporate virtual touch to create a metaverse world of your own. When it comes to metaverses, you are probably already aware of the concept if you have ever seen the *Ready Player One* movie. At the same time, virtual worlds are being envisioned and constructed with the assistance of improved artificial intelligence, the implementation of universal standards, and the ever-increasing performance of computer processing power. You and your children will be able to visit metaverses, making today's internet appear as if it were a silent movie compared to the internet of tomorrow.

NFTs will be a critical component of metaverses, serving as the basic components for assets that may be used in any of these worlds, regardless of where they are located. As you create your virtual house, you will fill the walls with original NFT art and "prints" of replicated visual art that you have purchased from collectors to decorate it. Then you host a gathering of friends in your immersive digital home, where they can enjoy the music you've collected and admire your NFT art, which now symbolizes not just a creator's original work but also its history and the tale of how you came to be the proud owner of that art piece. Your pals come in an instant, without the use of fossil fuels or the need for an Uber. You may have been disappointed that they didn't stop all along the way to pick up chips, but they offered new digital clothing for your avatar as a housewarming present.

Metaverse will become more integrated with the actual world due to NFTs. Exact locations will have digital equivalents in virtual space, and NFT art galleries will exist in the physical world and on digital screens. Music performances will be staged in a concert hall and a virtual bar, to name a few examples. These NFTs will be sold to you as part of your virtual library of concert tickets, which will be displayed in your virtual house and include an e-signature/personalized greeting from the artist, which will be sent directly to you.

CHAPTER 3

NFT AND BLOCKCHAINS

NATHAN REAL

Chapter 3.
NFT AND BLOCKCHAINS

3.1 Blockchains

A blockchain is a decentralized software network that serves as a digital record and a platform for the safe transfer of funds without requiring a third party to act as an intermediary. Like how the internet supports the digital information flow, blockchain is a distributed ledger that keeps the digital exchange of units of value in the same way that the internet promotes the movement of information. On a blockchain network, anything from currency to land titles to voting may be tokenized, recorded, and transferred, and this includes votes themselves.

The Bitcoin, a peer-to-peer electronic currency system that is safe, censorship-resistant, and decentralized, was the first embodiment of blockchain technology, appearing in 2009. Bitcoin is an open or permission-less blockchain model since it is available to anybody who wants to use it. There are several different types of blockchain technology available today. Several blockchains have been created to satisfy the demands of a small number of players, and network access is limited for these people. These are also instances of private blockchains.

Blockchain technology creates a permanent forensic record of every transaction and a single version of the truth, in addition to ensuring the safe movement of currency. This network state is completely visible and exhibited in real-time for the advantage of all players. However, irrespective of the nature of the implemented blockchain network, blockchain technology holds great promise for transforming nearly a century-old business models, laying the groundwork for higher levels of credibility in government, and opening up new avenues for economic opportunity for everyday citizens.

The unique identification and possession of an NFT may be verified via blockchain ledger technology. The NFT is often coupled with a permit to use the fundamental digital asset. In most cases, the buyer does not get ownership of the underlying digital asset. In some instances, permissions are exclusively granted for individual, non-commercial use, and in other cases, licenses are also given for commercial use of the actual digital asset

3.2 Digital Art

Due to the blockchain's capacity to ensure the unique identifier and ownership of NFTs, digital art was one of the first applications for NFTs to emerge. As I said before, in 2021, the artist Mike Winkelmann (better known by his stage name Beeple) sold a digital artwork named *Everydays: the First 5000 Days* for US$69.3 million, the highest price ever paid for a computer artwork. It was the third-highest auction price ever achieved as a living artist, behind only pieces by Jeff Koons & David Hockney, who each earned $1 million.

Blockchain has also been used for the public registration and authentication of existent physical artworks to distinguish them from counterfeit and certify their ownership via the use of physical trackers or labels, among other applications. In March 2021, Nifty Gateway sold another Beeple work, Crossroad, a ten-second movie depicting animated people just going past a depiction of Donald Trump, and the item sold for US$6.6 million.

In the Post-War to Current auction at Christie's, Curio Cards, a digital collection of 30 unique cards thought to be the 1st NFT art collector's items on the Ethereum network, sold for $1.2 million, thus making the NFT most expensive art collectible ever sold. The lot also included the card "17b," which was a digital "printing error."

The EtherRocks and CryptoPunks collections, among others, are instances of generative art. A wide variety of pictures may be made by combining a selection of basic visual components in various configurations.

3.3 Blockchain Standards

Token standards were developed to accommodate a wide range of blockchain-based applications. Ethereum, with its ERC-721 average, was the first network to allow non-fungible tokens (NFTs), and it is presently the most extensively utilized. Because of the increasing popularity of NFTs, several other blockchains have incorporated or intend to add support for them.

Ethereum

ERC-721 was the first protocol for expressing digital assets that are non-fungible on the Ethereum blockchain, and it is the most widely used even today. Rigidity smart contract standard ERC-721 is inheritable, which means that developers may construct new ERC-721-compliant deals by importing existing ERC-721-compliant contracts from the Open Zeppelin library. When an asset has a unique identity, ERC-721 offers fundamental methods that enable the owner to be tracked down and provide permission means to transfer the item or purchase to others. The ERC-1155 standard provides "semi-fungibility," as well as a superset of the capabilities provided by the ERC-721 standard. In contrast to ERC-721 tokens, which have a unique ID representing a single asset, ERC-1155 tokens have a unique ID representing a class of support, with an extra quantity field to reflect the amount of a specific class wallet has. Transferring assets between types is possible, and the user may move any number of assets between classes at any point in time.

The present high transaction costs (also known as gas fees) associated with Ethereum have prompted the development of layer 2 solutions for the cryptocurrency, which also allow NFTs:

- A layer 2 network for Ethereum created exclusively for NFTs; Immutable X uses ZK rollups to remove gas expenses from transaction fees, allowing it to be used with other NFT protocols.

- A proof-of-stake network originally referred to as the Matic Network. Polygon is backed by major NFT markets such as OpenSea and is a fork of the Ethereum blockchain.

Different Blockchains

- It is likely to buy and sell NFTs using Bitcoin Cash, which is the currency that drives the Jungle NFT exchange.

- Including its March 2021 update, Cardano added native tokens that allow for the construction of NFTs without the need for smart contracts. CNFT and Theos are two of Cardano's NFT markets.

- Proof of stake consensus mechanism, the Flow blockchain, enables NFTs. There are plans to transition from ETH to Flow in the coming future for CryptoKitties.

- Powered by GoChain, the "eco-friendly" blockchain, the Zeromint NFT marketplace, and the VeVe app run on GoChain.

- Non-fungible tokens are supported by the Solana blockchain as well.

- It is a proof-of-stake blockchain network that facilitates the selling of NFT art and is known as "Tezos."

Off-Chain Storage

Due to the file's size, most NFTs incorporating digital art do not save it on the blockchain. The token operates more like a certification of ownership, along with a website address referring to the work of art in issue, implying that the work of art is still vulnerable to link rot. Because NFTs are functionally distinct from the base artworks, anybody may readily save a copy of the picture of an NFT, most often with a right-click. NFT supporters dismiss this copying of NFT artistry as a "right-clicker mindset," with one collector equating the value of a bought NFT to that of a symbol of status "to demonstrate how they can afford to spend that much."

The expression "right-clicker mindset" quickly gained popularity after its debut, notably among those skeptical of the NFT marketplace, who used it to demonstrate the ease with which digital art supported by NFT could be captured. Geoffrey Huntley, an Australian programmer, reinforced this critique when he constructed "The NFT Bay," a clone of The Pirate Bay. The NFT Bay marketed a torrent file containing 19 gigabytes of NFT digital art. Huntley likened his endeavor to a Pauline Pantsdown art piece and hoped that the site would educate visitors about what NFTs are and aren't.

3.4 Use of Blockchain by NFTs

NFTs provide the capacity to assign/claim ownership of any one-of-a-kind piece of digital data that can be tracked using Ethereum's network as a public ledger, allowing anybody to participate in the digital economy. A non-fungible token (NFT) is a digital entity that may depict digital or non-digital assets.

NFTs are rapidly all-encompassing over the world of digital art and collectibles, and for a good reason. Digital artists are witnessing a transformation in their livelihood because sales are being made to a new audience. Celebrities are also hopping on board to see a unique chance to connect with their followers. Nevertheless, digital art is just one use of NFTs. Realistically, they may be used to symbolize possession of any exclusive object, such as an action for property in either the physical or digital world.

If Andy Warhol were born in the late 1990s, he would almost certainly have coined Campbell's Soup as a non-fungible token.

3.5 Concerns About the Environment

In the context of blockchain transactions, the purchase and sale of NFTs are embroiled in a debate concerning the high energy consumption and resulting greenhouse gas emissions connected with such transactions.

In particular, the proof-of-work mechanism is necessary to govern and validate the transactions. Estimating the environmental footprint of a provided NFT transaction requires making several assumptions about how that specific NFT transaction is set up on a blockchain, the economic behavior of blockchain miners (as well as the energy needed of their mining equipment), as well as the quantity of renewable energy that is being used on these networks. Other questions concern the nature of the carbon footprint estimates for NFT purchases, such as whether the estimated carbon footprint for an NFT purchase should consider some portion of the currently underway energy needs of the underlying network or only the marginal effect of that particular purchase. For this, an analog has been provided in the high carbon footprint connected with an extra passenger on a specific airline trip.

Newer NFT systems include alternative validation methods like proof of stake, which need much less energy for a particular validation cycle than traditional protocols. More techniques to reduce power use include online transactions as part of the minting process for a non-fungible token. A couple of NFT art sites are also attempting to address these problems, with some opting to use technologies and protocols with smaller environmental footprints. Others are now offering the opportunity to purchase carbon offsets while making NFT purchases, albeit the ecological advantages have been called into doubt. NFT artists have decided not to sell part of their very own work to reduce their carbon emission commitments in certain circumstances.

Because NFTs are becoming more popular, they are also becoming the subject of heightened scrutiny, particularly regarding their carbon impact.

To be clear on a few points:

- Non-fungible tokens (NFTs) do not directly contribute to the carbon output of Ethereum.

- Ethereum's method of keeping your dollars and assets safe is now energy-intensive, but it is on the verge of becoming less so.

- Once it has been enhanced, Ethereum's carbon output will be 99.95% lower, making it more energy-efficient than many other sectors now in use.

3.6 Blockchains Supporting NFTs

Since its introduction in the mid-2010s, non-fungible tokens (NFTs) had seen a surge in popularity, which peaked in February 2021 when Beeple's *Everydays NFT* was sold for a world-record-breaking $69.3 million.

Since then, NFTs have gained widespread acceptance and are now available for purchase on various online marketplaces and backed by several different blockchains.

List of the most famous blockchains compatible with NFTs other than Ethereum network:

Zilliqa

Zilliqa, which was launched in 2017, is the world's first-ever public sharding-based blockchain, according to the company. Zilliqa is meant to be more resilient regarding scalability, which means

that network expansion does not influence transaction performance. Early blockchains, such as Bitcoin and Ethereum, were
infamous for the slowness they processed transactions.

Flow

Proof-of-stake blockchain, Flow, is primarily built to serve NFTs
and other consumer-oriented applications. Dapper Labs, the
creators of CryptoKitties, among the first games based on NFTs,
developed Flow in response to the Ethereum network being clog-
ged due to CryptoKitties transactions in 2017.

Tezos

Tezos is a proof-of-stake blockchain introduced in 2018 and is
open-source software. Tezos fosters involvement and coopera-
tion with the users for continuous improvement and long-term
upgradeability due to its open-source nature. Compared to Ethereum, Tezos stresses many advantages, the most notable of which
is its eco-friendliness, since it requires 2 million times less power
and much less than 1 XTZ to mint 1 NFT than Ethereum.

Solana

According to its developers, Solana is a proof-of-stake blockchain
that promises to be the quickest in the world. Unquestionably,
one of the most attractive characteristics of Solana is its capacity
to scale, which ensures that the network will always be speedy
while also guaranteeing that on the web, no transaction will ever
surpass $0.01.

Cardano

Cardano is a blockchain that operates on the proof-of-stake principle and is open-source. It has a formidable team behind it, including the Ethereum co-founder, and it emphasizes the necessity of regulatory compliance and scalability in its development.
It also promises to become the most ecologically friendly blockchain technology available.

CHAPTER 4

WHAT ARE SOME OF THE MOST POPULAR NFTS?

NATHAN REAL

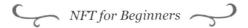

Chapter 4.
WHAT ARE SOME OF THE MOST POPULAR NFTS?

Non-fungible tokens (NFTs) have been widely used in digital money because they may be used to convey information uniquely while maintaining ownership of the data.

In turn, they've progressed beyond what we might expect from a digital token as a simple measure of wealth, becoming a collectible item with an endless variety of heads, as B. Allen explains: "Folks adore to collect things, whether it's sporting events cards, bottle caps, or matchbooks; NFTs satisfy this desire without taking up physical space." Aside from that, they also offer a substantial potential upside, meaning that a $100 purchase might potentially turn into $1,000 there in the future, comparable to investing in the secondary art market. Given the fact that NFTs are a cutting-edge innovation, they appeal to people who are willing to break the mound and attempt something new and exciting." The well-known nature of NFTs has been employed to create single and engaging viewers' experiences in other media. Robert Alice's NFT, which was produced in collaboration with Alethia.AI, was recently sold off by Sotheby's and the New York Foundation for the Arts. FAMILY has unveiled its BoringStone Genesis Collection, part of a wider NFT project that includes members of the greater NFT community as participants.

According to L. Rensing, founder and chairman of enterprise bitcoin solutions provider Protokol, the popularity of NFTs in the sports and entertainment space provided an opportunity to participate with fans at a time when traditional avenues for doing so were closed due to the pandemic: "The prominence of NFTs in the sports and entertainment room offered a chance to engage in fanning base at a time when conventional lines of inquiry for doing so were shuttered due to the pandemic."

So, from the Kings of Leon releasing their current album as an NFT to the success of NBA Greatest Shots and WePlay Esports' NFTs, it shows many athletes, video game teams, performers, and musicians jump into the ring to make their mark. If done correctly, NFTs have the potential to generate significant long-term growth while also increasing fan engagement. Issuers may be able to accomplish this by trying to make NFTs more than just digital collectibles, rather than simply offering them as individualized rewards for fan loyalty and participation.

4.1 The Emergence of NFTs

At the Token 2049 festival *NFTs: From Zero to One*, the visual artist spoke about her collaboration with S. Aoki and cited meme/gif society and political mainstream press as the quickest propulsion systems for the rising global popularity of NFTs. She added: "I'm excited about this collaboration. I believe that memes and gifs are a part of this process because they are the most efficient means of spreading information. When users consider a marketing strategy, each time a few of these memes/gifs is effective, you will see it and have the opportunity to use it."

To summarize, "creating an effective meme requires anticipating the NFTs hit rate among normal people and relying on a small amount of luck or chance, which no one can comprehend; this is the most difficult aspect of the process. So sometimes a meme starts, but other times it's completely random, and this is why I believe it's highly beneficial to analyze what others do and watch, and it may be the most effective tool for people to publicize; the foundation of an electronic token market, to name a few examples" according to the author.

Among the most appealing characteristics of NFTs is their ability to keep the owner's true identity, which distinguishes them as a contemporary step forward in the evolution of the art world. According to Bradley Miles, CEO as well as co-founder of Roll's, "NFTs is an early demonstration of how both the artist and the users may economically hold the content. They are reversing the traditional ownership model. Ownership of the content or item remains solely with the creator, and the platform is only a method for the user to show, trade, or otherwise make use of what they have created. Even though NFTs are a unique paradigm, they are fundamentally aligned with artists in that they provide them with more economic control over the content they create on the internet."

According to H. Sheikh, "one of the reasons why NFTs make owning digital art so enticing is the element of genuineness it provides. It has fundamentally altered the way we defend our digital intellectual property rights." Like V. Pestritto, Partner Programs Manager of Agoric, notes, "NFTs are a coupled business reason to a marketplace that loves the idea of irreparable ownership. In the past few weeks, I've met small business owners who are also art collectors. They're purchasing non-traditional works of art because of the evident relevance and culture associated with owning art. People who work in the crypto industry as artists and depend on their day jobs to finance their passion have identified a clear opportunity to reach out now to crypto enthusiasts who recognize the unique feature of the NFT/artwork developed."

4.2 Value of NFTs

Even though NFTs allow people to represent, store, and trade their resources, do they have any lengthy value? NFTs are distinguished from other collectibles by the possibility of an unexpected financial failure. The value of an NFT is determined by the public's perception of its worth, including its exclusivity and rarity. D. Weragoda, MBANC's CTO (Chief Technology Officer), explains that "most individuals don't comprehend the key technical NFTs, or even what NFTs is, and you'll have to comprehend what you're entering into before you start spending money into hyped-up illusions."

However, this type of conduct has led many individuals to lose money in other financial markets, such as Bitcoin. "Be careful when tying non-fungible tokens to anything that provides true use, since what exactly are you buying in? The fact that it's a new child on the block means that there's a massive industry for buzzwordy technology. Since we all understand, the bitcoin has a very short attention span," H. Sheikh writes on evaluating the actual price of an NFT if there are no tangible criteria to justify the pricing of the NFT. Given the rapid shift in public opinion, if the thing is to be used as a measure of wealth, it is necessary to identify the criteria by which the item's worth will be assessed in the future.

The NFT has "a sense of worth," but it is impossible to attribute a genuine value to it without first understanding where the true value derives from. Consequently, the current pattern is no longer viable in the long run. If non-fungible tokens (NFTs) are used to prove ownership of property riches, like real estate, they will become a feasible trend. The community's evaluation of whether or not a specific NFTs' value will continue to climb decides whether or not that asset is regarded as a desirable item in the first place. There has to be a more quantitative technique for estimating a non-fungible token's future value.

4.3 Perspectives for the Future

It is estimated that the increase around the world in NFTs more than doubled in the short time between July and August 2021, surpassing 1.3 million unique buyers and sellers, according to Statista figures. Recently released data from NonFungible.com revealed that NFT sales reached between $10 million and $20 million per week, with weekly transaction volume increasing by approximately 300% during various times of the year. Is the increasing popularity of NFTs here to remain, or will they be a relic of the past shortly?

According to Brittany Allen, who is concerned about their long-term survival, considering that NFTs are still in their infancy, it's hard to predict what form they will take in the future. "After subsequent buys of NFTs start to earn value—or at the very least sustain interest—I believe they will become a permanent fixture in the financial landscape. There would inevitably be failures along the way," she goes on to say.

"In the case of early adult literature, for example, once literature Twitter was revealed to be infringing on the copyrights of children, this NFT attempt failed, highlighting the necessity of investors making educated judgments at such a young point in the industry's lifespan. Numerical fractions are all here to live, and their use will continue to expand inside the art world, into artist collaborations and assistance for secondary market transactions, and outside the art world, into other unique scenarios for businesses," Vanessa Pestritto expresses herself. NFTs for small businesses can generate a more trustworthy link between transacting parties in various situations, including commercial invoices, theater tickets, and printing more money in the case of projects and collaboration. However, James K. Cropcho advises against adopting NFTs to earn quick money in the near term: "NFTs is both a trend and something that will be there for a long time." Nevertheless, because NFTs are a novel and, as a result, "bright and new" item, many individuals who would not normally collect have experimented in the industry; however, many of them are likely searching for quick cash to supplement their income. However, even though several periodicals and news shows have covered the matter, usually with a disdainful air of goofiness rather than an attempt at serious explication, NFTs are not widely accepted. Based on pure speculation, I assume that the global market for NFTs is less than the global market for jellyfish.

4.4 Popular NFTs

Over the past several generations, non-fungible tokens have become a popular financial notion. While many uses for these bitcoin assets are still in the early stages of development, art investment has surfaced as an initial NFT success story. Traditional art investment was mostly reserved for the rich, but non-fungible tokens (NFTs) have opened up art purchasing and selling to the public. There are a few and far between ideas you need to be familiar with before getting started, one of which is what the greatest NFT art presently looks like. They are excellent investments in which to gain money.

CryptoPunks

CryptoPunks were 10,000 one-of-a-kind pixelated pictures of a varied range of characters created by Larva Labs. The blockchain-based art effort Larva Labs was among the earliest NFT art successes, and it was based on Ethereum's blockchain. The CryptoPunk program, first made available for free in 2017, has since gained widespread attention on social media. Paintings resold for millions of dollars have been a common occurrence.

Beeple

Mike Winkelman, better known by his alias Beeple, is a very well New Frontiers of Technology artist. In actuality, Christie's sold it off NFT-based artwork *Everydays: The First 5,000 Days* of even more than $69 million in March 2021, assisting in bringing NFT artwork into the public's attention for the first time. Beeple has been publishing a digital photo every day for more than 13 years, so his new work is in high demand, commanding high prices.

Bored Ape Yacht Club

It is a collection of 10,000 ape pictures from comic books that the author created. Each piece functions as a collector's item and an online membership card, granting owners access to a virtual environment designed specifically for the ape avatar. Even if the NFTs are sold out, you may still purchase them from owner-occupiers via an NFT market such as OpenSea. Huge sums of cash have previously been spent on the company's most expensive BAYCs.

Axie Infinity

Axie Infinite would be a bitcoin computer game created on the Ethereum platform and is available for download. Player's usage of Axies, fanciful animals that can be taught, bred to produce more Axies, and acquired and sold using Axie Shards, is utilized to participate in various tournaments. Hundreds and thousands of users log on to play Axie Infinity every day, and the most precious Axies may fetch thousands of dollars on the Ethereum cryptocurrency market. Pokémon-themed non-fungible token (NFT) videogame established on the Ethereum blockchain, Axie Infinity, is inspired by the mythology of the Pokémon franchise. Millions of Axies, attractive fantasy creatures can be raised, battled, and skilled as digital pets, which users may acquire, nurture, battle, and skill. Its primary idea is "play-to-earn," according to which gamers are compensated for the time and effort they put in. These advantages are provided in the form of an SLP coin, which you may acquire via normal gaming activities. Axie Infinity is possibly the best cryptocurrency concept ever conceived. Everything is built and refined from the user experience to tokenomics with meticulous attention to detail. It is presently the costliest NFT series, with a market value of $42 million in 2021, with sales of a further $1 billion per year expected for the following year. It works with various platforms, including Windows, Macintosh, iOS, and Android. To do this, they want to create a virtual market where people can own and manage enterprises while also saving, trading, and consuming payments without traveling to a bank.

Gods Unchained

Developers may access decks and participate in a game against one another in this free and easy-to-play trading card game. Gods Unchained seems to be a trading card game in the manner of Magic the Gathering. Because of its great in-game components and creative animations, every statement on the presidential website has increased to $1.3 million in less than a month, a significant increase from the previous month. Because the cards are verifiable property in Ethereum, all parties have ownership of their assets. Griffith, The Chosen, is an NFT card that appears in an instance. Gods Unchained seems to be the leading supplier of card game games, thanks to a freshly launched marketplace and a plethora of exchange options that are more extensive than ever.

CryptoKitties

CryptoKitties was the first game to be established on the Ethereum network, and it remains to this day. Player's purchase, sell and breed kittens to develop desired traits represented by ERC-721 coins that are inseparable and one-of-a-kind in the game. On big NFT exchanges like opensea.io, CryptoKitties may be traded for a profit. Dapper Labs developed the game published in November 2017 on the Ethereum blockchain. Believe it or not, acquiring and caring for digital cats seems interesting to engage in. The popularity of the game, for example, resulted in congestion and the creation of national heads on the Ethereum network in 2017. It is possible to get a CryptoKitty by buying one off the market. Pairing allows individuals to get access to otherwise unavailable skills. In addition, you may win incentives by building a collection of cat figurines. Once you've amassed a large enough supply of cats, you may transfer them to the KittyVerse, where they can engage in catfights. You will also be able to team up with a group to answer puzzles if you so want.

Illuvium

It is a user-friendly role-playing adventure game with a play-to-earn design that enables players to win in-game rewards as they play. You benefit from gas charges, peer-to-peer inventing, and fast operations, all while preserving safe control over your cash and cryptocurrency. Classic role-playing game elements are combined with combat strategies established by the Autobattler genre to provide a unique gaming experience. The Illuvium video game will be made available to the public in 2022.

The Sandbox

It is a virtual metaverse in which you may own property, participate in games, and even develop your own game from scratch. Govern the huge virtual world as a collector, creator, or game judge, or simply as a player that rambles about the metaverse, moving from one game to another, if you so want. Sandbox is a virtual world established on the Ethereum platform with its currency dubbed Sand. A blockchain editor has been developed, which may be used to construct pieces and simulations for bitcoin's future edition. One of the finest games to be played if you own these digital land and real estate while also having a large presence in the metaverse is *The Elder Scrolls: Legends of the Fallen*.

4.5 Buzzwords for NFTs

At their most basic level, most NFTs are Ethereum blockchain components. Ethereum is a cryptocurrency, like Bitcoin and Dogecoin. These NFTs, on the other hand, are enabled by blockchain, which holds additional information that allows them to operate only on an ETH token. It's worth noting that various blockchains may use NFTs in multiple ways. Although NFTs may be digitized (sketches, music, or even your mind being transported and transformed into an AI), the present buzz is on using technology to market digital art. As a result, I've put up a dictionary of NFT words.

PFP

"Profile picture" is abbreviated as PFP. PFP is responsible for the CryptoPunks, Meebits, beautiful kittens, and other avatars designs we use like Twitter and Discord profile photos.

DYOR

"DYOR" is an abbreviation that translates for "Do Your Own Research." This remark is commonly used when avoiding responsibility for the issue of whether an NFT is good or harmful for you.

HODL

It is a wrong spelling of "hold" that refers to acquiring goods practices in the world of cryptocurrency and NFTs.

In a panic, sell

In contrast to holding, anxious buyers get agitated when prices fall and rush to sell whatever they've bought. A minimal cost on NFT marketplaces, the least available list price is for the whole collection rather than a piece of the series.

Metaverse

Customers may interact with a device environment and other users via the metaverse, a virtualization technique. In essence, this is the web of tomorrow.

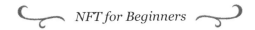

Purchase the Dip

When a cryptocurrency's price decreases, purchase it to benefit when the price climbs again.

Derivatives

Adapted from the original projects made famous by various "alternative" punks. They have little resemblance to the initial efforts. Art that is made on the spur of the moment. Algorithmically made art, preferably in real-time as it is coined.

FOMO

FOMO (Fear Of Missing Out) is the fear of losing out on something significant. Buying an NFT ensures that you don't miss out on another big thing.

Ethereum

Ethereum is a decentralized, open-source blockchain that enables users to build smart contracts. Ethereum is perhaps the most popular blockchain, especially among non-fungible tokens (NFTs). Ethereum is an excellent place to begin learning about this intriguing topic. They manage a large number of games. You'll discover something that interests you. Ethereum has blazed the way both with the NFT economy and the game CryptoKitties. You'll find a weblog and NFT activity monitoring data on this site. The cryptocurrency Ether (ETH) seems to be a digital asset.

The Ethereum cable network's initial cryptocurrency, Ether (ETH), is the second most popular digital token after Bitcoin (BTC). There are two sorts of ERCs: ERC-1155 and ERC-721.

Inside a single ERC-721 contract, only one token may be generated. Inside a single ERC-1155 contract, you may create many tickets.

Free for Gas

You must pay a fee to use the blockchain network. Two examples are giving funds from your account, interacting with a dap, trading tokens, or buying a collection. It's possible to think of it as a monthly cost. This price will vary based on how congested the network is because the mining in charge of completing your transactions is more likely to prioritize transactions with higher fees. The price rises as a result of congestion. Your pricing is decided by the quantity of gas needed for your payment on a technical level. Gas is the fee miners pay to generate extra data on a blockchain.

Metadata

Metadata is a set of data that uniquely defines your virtual model. The author, file size, time the site was produced, and keywords that describe the content may all be included in the metadata of an article. Metadata for just a sound file consists of the original artist, the album, and the year the music was released.

MetaMask

MetaMask is perhaps the most widely used non-custodial bank, which means you have complete control over your cash at all times. Unlike the other crypto wallets, MetaMask is built with privacy in mind. It enables you to acquire, keep, and trade tokens without having to worry about dApps or markets accessing more data than you've permitted them to. If you're using Defi applications or browsing Web 3.0 sites, MetaMask keeps you in absolute control of personal assets and data.

DAO

Decentralized Autonomous Organizations or DAOs are member-owned communities with no centralized leadership. Its goal is to empower an NFT marketplace's society and give governance via voting rights for platform improvements and moderation.

CryptoKitties

When the ICO raced and this game crowded the network, Crypto-Kitties remembered the horror and the delight. Everyone selected to possess an alpha cat rallying call or a rare one to make money. Assumption and materialism drove individuals to purchase such assets. The goal was to make money. There's nothing wrong with it. CryptoKitties came up with a great use case. CryptoKitties' creation of gaming with such a cryptocurrency overlay will go down in history. NFT will add another dimension to how you spend your time playing those games. You'll now devise a financial motivation, and your work will gain worth as you acquire helpful cards and stuff over time. Perhaps, individuals will earn a full-time income from the NFT economy in the not-too-distant future. It may be closer than we believe! The hitch with non-fungible tokens is that they are about to strike the betting industry like a storm. Consider getting money every week from NTF by selling, accumulating, or trading value. In the crypto world, this is another amazing aspect of the blockchain.

CHAPTER 5

HOW DOES NFT WORK?

NATHAN REAL

Chapter 5.
HOW DOES NFT WORK?

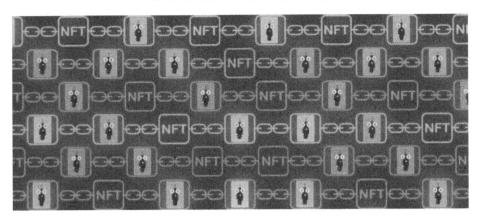

You've undoubtedly heard of words like Bitcoin, blockchain, and, more recently, NFTs if you've been following the tech headlines lately. Artists & collectors alike have been drawn to stories of mega-dollar auctions for digital assets. But what exactly are NFTs? Also, how do they function? We'll look at the fundamentals of non-fungible tokens, cryptocurrency technology that underpins them, and how they're used in daily life. We'll also go over certain skills and expertise you'll need to join them.

The term "non-fungible token" refers to a not-fungible token. That probably doesn't imply anything at this point; the word "fungible" isn't used all that much. It does, however, imply that anything is replaceable.

Money, for example, is just a fungible asset in economics, and it is divided into units that can be readily swapped without gaining or losing value. Gold, cryptocurrencies, and stocks are all examples of fungible assets.

As we learned in the cryptocurrency open step, a fungible asset can be divided up in various ways and infinite quantities. They may be used for multiple purposes, including payments and storing value.

The non-fungible asset, on either hand, is a one-of-a-kind item, such as a painting, a home, or a trading card. Even though an artwork may be replicated or filmed, the source is the original, and reproductions are not valuable.

NFTs are electronic information units that are stored on the blockchain. Each non-fungible token acts as an authentication certificate, proving that a digital item is unique and not interchangeable. Because of the cryptographic concepts that make blockchain unique, an NFT is never modified, amended, or stolen.

5.1 Blockchain

We've written a comprehensive guide on blockchain, cryptocurrencies, and bitcoin. We said in that piece that a blockchain is a database, a compilation of electronically recorded information or data. Unlike a traditional database, a blockchain comprises corresponding data "blocks." This blockchain chain forms a shared information ledger (data collection) that records the chain's activities and information.

Each blockchain database is kept on hundreds of separate servers worldwide. It implies that everybody on the network may see (and confirm) everyone else's entries. It's practically hard to falsify or meddle with data inside a block using this peer-to-peer & distributed ledger technology. So, according to IBM, blockchain is a distributed, irreversible (permanent and unalterable) database that makes recording transactions and monitoring assets easier. When we conceive NFTs, we think of them as being produced on a blockchain, never being transferred to another blockchain environment. It will live on the blockchain and serve as proof of the validity of the item you bought.

5.2 Digital Asset

Simply said, a digital asset is everything that exists in digital form and could be used (a right to duplicate, copy, modify, reproduce, and otherwise use). Documents, audio or video information, photographs, and other related digital data, for example, are all termed digital assets.

5.3 Why Are NFTs Worthy?

As we've previously discussed, a non-fungible item is a license of possession for a digital asset. The value is obtained from the property's collectability and potential future selling value, and NFTs may be bought and sold.

Using art as an illustration of the gains of NFTs is a further superb example.

NFT Auctions Standards

The art of the NFT was not the only item that sold. Recently, there have been some large sales in NFTs, expressing concern that the economy has been in a bubble. The following are some instances of NFT sales:

- It is the first Tweet. Twitter's creator, Jack Dorsey, sold his NFT during his first Tweet worth $2.9 million.

- The "Nyan Cat" animated GIF. The NFT again for bright GIF was marketed for 300 Ethereum, worth almost $561,000 just at the time.

- *Charlie Bit Me* video. A video of a baby eating his brother's fingers was seen over 800 million hours on YouTube. The NFT of the video was sold for around £500,000.

5.4 What Can You Do with Non-Fungible Tokens?

Many people wonder whether there are any applications for NFTs. Even though the notion is still in its infancy, numerous possible applications have already developed. Below, we've selected a handful of the more notable ones:

Ticket

Event tickets are one of the applications of NFTs that we described in our first step. The argument is if tickets are produced that use a non-fungible token, there will be a record of that trade if the key is exchanged.

Therefore, there is no possibility of scalping, stealing, or attempting to use counterfeit tickets. Hence, the token on the blockchain linked with that ticket cannot be replaced.

Fashion

NFTs have the potential to solve several important difficulties in the fashion industry. To begin with, maintaining a permanent copy of authenticity aids in the detection of counterfeit items. An NFT might be connected to a luxury object to prove its authenticity. Likewise, a non-fungible token might provide important information about an item's origins, such as the components used, where they came from, and how far it has traveled. It might help individuals make more ethical judgments as topics like design and conservation are more prominent.

Collectables

We've previously touched on this subject. Collecting souvenirs, trinkets, and other such stuff has long been a popular pastime. NFTs act as electronic signatures or seals of approval, confirming authenticity.

Gaming

We looked at the massive market value associated with gaming in our piece on the video game business. NFTs allow players to possess one-of-a-type in-game objects, and such tokens may fuel in-game ecosystems, whether for enjoyment, authenticity, or competitive nature.

5.5 Working

Paintings, as well as other traditional pieces of art, are prized for their uniqueness. On either hand, digital files may be easily or endlessly replicated. Graphics may be "tokenized" using NFTs to generate a digital proof of purchase that can be purchased and sold. Will physical trading cards be phased out in favor of digital-only trade cards? A track of who owns what, like crypto-currency, is kept on a public ledger blockchain network. So, because multiple computers keep ledgers all around the globe, the data cannot be fabricated. NFTs may also include smart contracts that, for example, offer the artist a percentage of any future token sales.

NFTs differ from ERC-20 tokens like DAI & LINK in that every ticket is one-of-a-kind and cannot be split. NFTs allow for the assignment or claim of possession of any individual data subject's data, which let be trailed using Ethereum's network as a shared ledger. As a portrayal of digital, non-digital properties, an NFT is created from digital items. An NFT possibly will, for standard, signify:

Art in the Digital Age:

- GIFs
- Collectibles

- Music
- Videos

An item from the real world:

- Deeds to a vehicle

- Tickets to a live event in the real world

- Invoices that have been tokenized

- Documents of legal significance

- Signatures

There is a surplus of new options to explore!

At any moment, an NFT can have one owner. The unique information that no other tokens can reproduce is used to maintain ownership. Smart contracts which assign proprietorship & govern the NFTs are utilized to produce them. When someone generates or mints an NFT, they execute code from clever agreements that follow various standards, including ERC-721. This data is stored on the blockchain, where the NFTs are handled. From a high level, the minting process includes the subsequent steps:

- Add together a different tower block to the match

- Knowledge verification

- Containing files against the blockchain

NFTs have a few exceptional characteristics:

- Each token has a unique identification tied to a single Ethereum address.

- They are not replaceable 1:1 with other tokens. 1 ETH, for example, is identical to another ETH, and with NFTs, this isn't the case.

- Each coin has a unique owner whose identity can be readily verified.

- They are based on Ethereum and may be purchased and traded on every Ethereum-based NFT exchange.

To put it a different way, if you acquire an NFT: It's simple to show that you own it. Demonstrating that you hold an NFT is comparable to showing that you also have ETH within your account.

Let's imagine you buy an NFT and have possession of the one-of-a-kind token transmitted to your wallet through your public address.

- The token verifies that your digital file copy is the original.

- Your private key serves as verification that you hold the original.

- The originator's public key is inextricably linked to the token's history. The creator's access policy may be used to prove that a certain person generated the ticket you own, increasing its market worth (vs. a counterfeit).

- Signing messages to confirm you possess the private key underlying the address is another technique to prove you still own NFT.

- It cannot be manipulated in any manner.

- You may resell it, and in certain situations, resale royalties will be paid to the original inventor.

- Alternatively, you may keep it indefinitely, safe in the knowledge that your Ethereum wallet will protect your investment.

Also, if you make an NFT:

- You may establish that you are the creator.

- You determine the scarcity.

- Every time it is sold, you may receive royalties.

- You may sell this on any NFT or peer-to-peer exchange. You're not attached to anyone's program, and you don't require any-

Nathan Real

body to act as an intermediary.

5.6 Scarcity

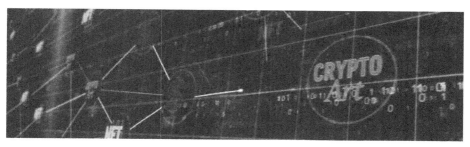

The developer of an NFT is in charge of determining the asset's scarcity. Consider purchasing a ticket to something like a sports event. The designer of an NFT may pick how many copies there are, much as an event organizer can choose how many tickets to sell. 5000 general admission tickets, for example, are sometimes exact reproductions. For example, a ticket with only an allocated seat may be issued in multiples that are extremely similar yet somewhat different. In another scenario, the designer could seek to construct a one-of-a-kind NFT as a unique collectible.

Each NFT might still have a distinct character (like a barcode system on a typical "ticket") and only one owner in these scenarios. The NFTs intended scarcity is important, and it is up to the designer to decide. A creator might intend to create each NFT fully unique to promote absence, or they may have good cause to generate thousands of copies. Keep in thinking that all this knowledge is available to the public.

5.7 Royalties

When certain NFTs are sold, royalties are automatically sent to the creators. It is a new notion, yet it's already among the most powerful. Every time an NFT is sold, the rightful owners of Euler Beats Founders get an 8% royalty. And certain sites, like Foundation and Zora, encourage their artists to earn royalties. It is automated, so authors can sit back to collect royalties as the work is passed across from one individual to the next. Currently, calculating royalties is exceedingly laborious and inaccurate, which means many artists are underpaid. You'll rarely miss out on a royalty if your NFT is configured with one.

5.8 Increasing Creators' Earnings

The most widespread use of NFTs currently is in digital material. Since the industry is in a country of confusion today, Boards are sapping content producers' income & earning potential. An illustrator who works on a social television site makes proceeds for the podium, advertising adverts to the performer's followers. In conversation, they get publicity, but coverage does not pay the bills.

NFTs firewood a new innovative financial system in which creators retain control of their work rather than distribute it to the platforms that promote it. Ownership is ingrained in the substance. Whenever they sell their work, the money goes straight to them. The original author may be entitled to royalties if the new owner sells the NFT. The creator's location is part of a token's information, which can't be changed. Therefore, this is assured every time it's sold.

5.9 Increasing Gameplay Opportunities

NFTs have piqued the curiosity of game developers. NFTs could be applied to monitor who owns what it is in, drive in-game economics, and provide a range of additional benefits to players.

Many regular games allow you to buy items to use in your game. However, if the weapon was an NFT, you may be able to recoup your commitment by purchasing it after the game. You may even make money if that item becomes more popular. Game designers may be royalty paid if an order is placed on the free market, consequently of their work on the NFT. Accordingly, a more mutually beneficial business model arises, in which the tertiary NFT market benefits both players and creators. It also indicates that even when the game's makers cease supporting it, the content you've amassed is yours to keep. In the end, the in-game objects you grind for may outlast the game itself, and your things will still be under your control, even if a sport is no longer supported. As a result, in-game artifacts become digital memorabilia with a value outside the game. Decentraland, a virtual world game, allows you to purchase NFTs that represent virtual land tracts as you want.

5.10 Working of Minting NFT

A few things must happen while minting an NFT:

- It proves that the proposed is a blockchain asset.

- The amount of the owner's account must be changed to accommodate that asset, allowing it to be exchanged or "owned" in a verifiable manner.

- The transactions, as mentioned earlier, must be added to brick & "immortalized" just on-chain.

Everybody in the network must agree that the block is "correct." Because of system decides to know your NFT originates and belongs to you, there is no need for intermediaries. It's also on the blockchain so that anybody can check it. One of the methods Ethereum assists NFT developers in maximizing their revenue is via this mechanism.

Miners oversee all these responsibilities. They also inform the entire network about their NFT and who owns it. It implies mining must be sufficiently tough; otherwise, anybody might claim possession of the NFT you just coined and transfer ownership unlawfully. There are several incentives put in place to ensure that miners operate honestly.

CHAPTER 6

HOW AND WHERE TO BUY NFTS?

NATHAN REAL

Chapter 6.
HOW AND WHERE TO BUY NFTS?

6.1 The NFTs

NFTs were the greatest crypto story of 2021, through Crypto-Punks to pet rocks. Though NFT marketplaces aren't quite as user-friendly as Amazon, purchasing your first digital collectible isn't difficult—it just takes a little coaching. It is how purchasing an NFT work, Fortnite decals are character decals that add no actual value to a gamer's gameplay, yet children worldwide ask their parents to spend loads of money on them so they can brag to their peers. Virtual property is a fairly new thing rapidly gaining traction, particularly among younger people. With the support of the blockchain, NFTs take digital property to the next level.

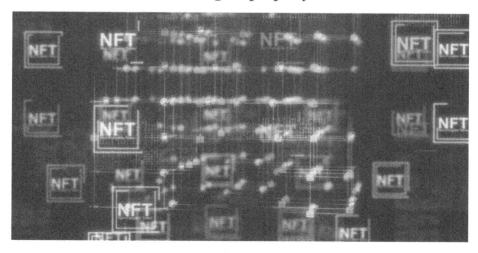

Before NFTs, virtual ownership was based on firms' centralized servers, which could be corrupted. Fortnite, for illustration, erased players' Travis Scott skins after the event at his concert, abandoning them without anything. The only way to own a digital object properly is to own it on a public blockchain; because a central authority does not manage NFTs, the actual ownership of these commodities is possible. Christie's Auction Site broke the distinction of being the largest selling non-fungible token (NFT) to history in March, with a transaction valued at over 69 billion dollars in Ethereum. NFTs are being used by artists such as Beeple to distribute digital paintings that can be certified as legitimate via the blockchain. The non-fungible tokens vary from some of the other crypto holdings in that they are not fungible. Unlike other cryptocurrencies, many of these tokens do not have value based on their usefulness.

Research Available NFTs

You should select an NFT that you believe has upward worth. The NFT might be a piece of art, music, film, or maybe even a console game item. NFTs may be found by searching Google or Twitter. Tools and NFTcatcher.io feature an up-to-date list of Ethereum and Solana NFTs soon launch. When searching at forthcoming NFTs, take note of something like the date of the auction, the crypto criteria, and the number of NFTs getting offered. It allows you to comprehend better the rarity of the NFT you've chosen. The group at the back of NFT and whether this is on-chain or off-chain are two things you should verify about something. Off-chain relies on centralized servers, meaning the picture will be destroyed if the site is down.

Select a Brokerage or Exchange to Purchase Crypto

To obtain the NFT, you must first purchase the coin. The majority of NFTs are acquired with Ethereum, with a few outliers. A dedicated crypto bank or market, such as Bitcoin (NASDAQ: COIN), Robinhood (NASDAQ: HOOD), Gemini, Binance.US, or Kraken, can help you acquire Ethereum and other cryptocurrencies. A cryptocurrency brokerage is a company or individual that acts as a middleman to help people acquire and exchange altcoins. An exchanger is a web-based marketplace where bidders trade depending on the prevailing market circumstances. When purchasing cryptocurrencies, please remember that charges are a significant consideration. For a transaction of $10 or less, Coinbase, for example, costs $0.99. The larger the deal, the higher the cost. For crypto trading, SoFi Active Invest costs up to 1.25%. Fees might be a fixed rate per transaction or a percentage of an account's 30-day trading volume. Examine costs depending on the deal sizes you want to undertake to determine how much you'll pay.

6.1 How to Buy NFTs?

Because most NFTs are cryptocurrency tokens, most NFT markets only take ETH tokens as payment. If you have a cryptocurrency profile, you may use it to buy Ethereum and transfer it to your MetaMask pocket. Coinbase and eToro are ideal alternatives for novices if you do not yet have a crypto trading membership. You'll want an Ethereum-compatible crypto wallet and enough ETH to get began. Purchase some ETH on an exchanger like Coinbase and deposit it in Coinbase Account (which is distinct from the primary Coinbase application and can be downloaded from the Download Page). There are several online markets where you may purchase and sell NFTs. You'll be able to afford to buy various forms of art or antiques depending on whatever marketplace you pick. Many of these platforms include supplementary storefronts with a range of NFTs, but each platform has its own set of rules. MetaMask is an Ethereum purse that can be accessed using a browser extension or a phone app. You'll have to have an Ethereum wallet to join OpenSea (and other NFT sites). Connect your MetaMask to a Ledger cryptocurrency wallet for optimum protection and reduce the chance of hacking. Copy MetaMask, create a wallet, then transmit the ETH you just bought from Coinbase over to it. Try out the complimentary Crypto & DeFi 101 tutorial for a video explanation if this is your initial time engaging with cryptocurrency wallets.

6.2 Where to Buy NFTs?

Token standards were developed to accommodate a wide range of blockchain-based applications. Ethereum, with its ERC-721 standard, was the first network to allow non-fungible tokens (NFTs), and it is presently the most extensively utilized. Because of the increasing popularity of NFTs, several other blockchains have incorporated or intend to add support for them.

OpenSea

OpenSea is always the greatest platform for buying and selling NFTs in the universe. The Ethereum, Polygon, and Klaytn blockchains are all supported. On this portal, you may search through over 34 million NFTs organized into thousands of genres, including visual art, antiques, gaming goods, virtual worlds, and web addresses. To join up for OpenSea, you'll want an Ethereum wallet like MetaMask, Coinbase Wallet, or Fortmatic, as well as a registration fee. Some NFT systems charge ahead for gas. The expenditure of completing transactions on a bitcoin network is called a gas charge. Because the NFT isn't transmitted on the blockchain until the transaction is complete, OpenSea allows developers to generate NFTs while incurring gas fees. That implies you may convert a digital version to an NFT for free and pay the price of natural gas after the item sells. After the NFT is sold, OpenSea additionally receives a 2.5% share. The consumers pay the cut on remedied products, whereas the seller pays it on auctioned items. On OpenSea, all activities are instantaneous, which implies either that the actual procedure or none of it transpires. And it's not like Amazon, where the customer must pay in advance for the products. As a result of the Wyvern Protocol, there is no difficulty with trust irrespective of who acts initially.

Axie Infinity

Axie Infinity is indeed a game's metaverse that players may develop and breed Axies, which they can then compete within a game called. Each Axie is a one-of-a-kind digital asset with its own set of characteristics that can be bought or sold. A MetaMask wallet must use Axie Infinity, developed on the Ethereum network. Before they can begin playing, new players must have at least 3 axes. You may not only trade in-game items for NFTs, but you can also purchase virtual property in the simulation.

Rarible

Another popular NFT auction for cryptocurrency photo editing is Rarible. You should have an Ethereum account to register on the platform. Photos, music, visual photography, subdomains, metaverses, and games are among the NFT genres available on Rarible. Certain NFTs are for sale at a specific price, including some sold. Maybe the most appealing feature of this system is the ability to earn royalties on the NFTs you resale, allowing you to generate a stream of passive income while still receiving a cut each time the NFT is sold. Rarible may also be used to earn prizes, which are rewarded out in Rarible's providing benefits, RARI coins. Rarible, like so many other forums, gets a

5% cut of each sale and divides it evenly between the consumer and the business. As a result, both sides must pay 2.5% of the total cost.

SuperRare

SuperRare links artists and collectors through a peer-to-peer digital art market. Yet, this is still in the beginning stages, and few musicians have signed on thus far. SuperRare is distinct in that it is limited to just those artists who match its requirements. You can submit your profile for evaluation if you wish to join the platform, and SuperRare will assess your profile based on some factors. It preserves its exclusivity by displaying artworks that are either or limited-edition items. Artists can mint and sell numerous renditions with the same picture on other NFT platforms. Users must have a MetaMask wallet to utilize SuperRare, which exclusively takes ETH payments. You'll have had to pay whichever the Ethereum show's gas charge is at the date of acquisition.

Mintable

Mintable is a gasless NFT platform in which you can mint NFTs from your memes, music, and streaming video. The premise is based on the Ethereum and Zilliqa blockchain systems, and registration requires a MetaMask wallet. Mintable gives you a MINT token per time you order an NFT. Like other NFT platforms, Mintable gets a percentage of every unit sold. It isn't, however, a fixed cost.

On the other hand, Mintable charges 2.5%, 5%, and 10% for standard, gasless, and reproducible NFTs, respectively. Mintable pays a royalty when you sell an NFT you originally occupied, although it isn't a set proportion. Alternatively, consumers may utilize the tiered system to select their desired royalty for all future revenue.

Nifty Gateway

Nifty Gateway, based on the Blockchain network, has become a community for professional artists. "Nifties" is the name given to the NFTs in this area. It's a platform where sole buyers are well-known singers and painters who've already bought dozens of nifties multimillion-dollar. In Feb 2021, for contrast, Beeple's *CROSSROAD* was purchased for even more than $6 million. Nifty Gateway isn't completely decentralized since web content is held on the network rather than the ledger. Every three days, a nifty is put up for sale. You can put in unsolicited bids, engage in lottery drawings, or bid in bids if you wish to acquire an NFT on Nifty Gateway. Credit cards can be applied to make acquisitions. On average, nifties have a high price tag, and painters receive a 10% commission across every selling.

Foundation

The basis is yet another NFT platform exclusively open to selected artists. However, unlike Nifty Gateway, it allows both undiscovered and well-known musicians to join the site. The Foundation's objective is to foster art by linking buyers and producers, and it is founded on the Ethereum platform. If you wish to sell NFTs on Foundation, you must fill out an application and provide a portfolio of your work. The Foundation will analyze your biography and offer you an appointment if your application is approved. You would need a MetaMask or Wallet Connect wallet unless you're a collector. The purchaser does not pay a commission to Foundation. It does, though, take a 15% commission on all sales. The platform's gas charge isn't set in stone and might fluctuate based on how often the system receives.

NBA Top Shot

Basketball Top Hit is the appropriate NFT marketplace for you if you're a sports fan. It allows NBA fans to swap digital experiences. For instance, if you watched a live NBA game and saw Stephen

Curry shoot a plink, you may mint it and sell it on NBA Best Shot. Users may accumulate NBA "memories" on the site. Sellers can post or remove things from the marketplace at no cost.

On the other hand, NBA Top Shot collects a 5% commission from every transaction. NFTs may be purchased with a virtual wallet or a bank card. If users pay in bitcoin, for example, ETH, the issuer's gas charge will be the same as the Ethereum channel's average gas fee.

What's the Right NFT Marketplace for You?

Selecting an assortment of NFT markets may be difficult, especially since there is no one-size-fits-all solution. The first stage is to establish your business scenario—what else are users searching for? What are your concerns? Do you wish to capture live match memories as a football fan? If that's the case, NBA Top Score is your best bet. Foundation and SuperRare would've been ideal for a skilled artist who wants a piece of a certain NFT industry. Axie Infinity, Verily, and Sorare are good options for gamers looking to join a gaming metaverse. Any prominent NFT market with cheap switching costs and unlimited NFT minting will suffice if you don't have a specialized business case in mind. After you've financed your account, purchasing an NFT is a simple process. Because most markets operate on an auction basis, you'll need to put a bid for the NFT you wish to buy. For NFTs with several prints, certain markets operate more like exchanges, employing the highest bid and lowest ask. One of the advantages is the possible resale value of an NFT purchased from the primary marketplace. Soon after release, some high-demand NFTs will sell 5–10 times their initial price. The disadvantage of purchasing NFTs in the secondary market is that it is difficult to predict demand. You may compare your purchase to past sales on the second-hand market.

Follow the easy steps to create your wallet, which serves as a haven for some of your cryptocurrency, a means of sending and receiving it, and a gateway to the ever-expanding world of crypto applications. From Rarible to Mintable, there's a slew of NFT marketplaces to choose from. For the sake of this lesson, we'll concentrate on OpenSea, which is the largest of them all and functions similarly to a decentralized eBay. To link your wallets to OpenSea, go to OpenSea.io. Get browsing! Prices range from essentially free to hundreds of thousands of dollars or more for a rare item. Some items are sold via auction, while others can be snagged immediately via a "buy now" button. Even though the NFT is free or inexpensive, you will still be charged to complete the purchase. The Ethereum network is used by most of the electronic assets on OpenSea, and the system levies a "gas" cost for events like NFT sales. The price of gas fluctuates according to how busy the system is. Select NFT that appeals to you and ensure that you have enough ETH to cover expenses. You may use your crypto wallet to retrieve the NFT once you've purchased it till you end up selling it.

NFTs are still basic, and so many analysts are unclear if they are a worthwhile investment. Although they use distributed ledger technology, it's unclear if the NFT will hold its benefits in the future. Investors should tread carefully. The four key elements determining the value are utility, ownership record, potential value, and liquidity bonus. The utility refers to utilizing it, such as a game token. If a well-known person or brand establishes the coin, large ownership values also have a role. The future value is based on a prediction of where the NFT will go in the year. The risk premium relates to how much demand is for the NFT, with greater premiums paid for NFTs with more traffic. An NFT can be exchanged for money or cryptocurrencies on the market. The chain records all events, protecting the NFTs' legitimate claim. Smart people invest in NFTs, which they feel will rise in value over time, then sell them again on a platform.

CHAPTER 7

HOW DO YOU CREATE NFTS?

NATHAN REAL

Chapter 7.
HOW DO YOU CREATE NFTS?

Today, NFTs are considered collectibles, and they're digital evidence of property that may be purchased and transferred over the internet. NFTs are stored on a blockchain, the same mechanism that powers cryptocurrencies and ensures that each asset is distinct. With this technique, altering or duplicating NFTs will become more challenging.

Before digging into NFTs, it's a good idea to grasp the economic concept of fungibility.

- **Fungible items:** Since their value isn't tied to their uniqueness, fungible things may be readily swapped. Although the new dollar's registration number is different, you can switch a $1 bill for another $1 note and still receive $1.

- **Non-fungible items:** Non-fungible items cannot be switched out. Each NFT coin has its own set of characteristics, but it does not have the same value as the other tokens that are the same.

So, why are individuals prepared to pay such a high amount for NFTs? "By establishing an NFT, creators may show uniqueness and validity to nearly anything digital," says Solo Ceesay. "There are innumerable reproductions of the Mona Lisa in existence, but still only one original. NFT technology is used to determine who possesses the original object."

7.1 NFTs and How They Work

Although the Ethereum system produces and stores up many NFTs, they are also accepted by other public blockchains (Flow and Tezos). Custody of the NFT could be readily authenticated and discovered thanks to the blockchain.

Digital items that may have been "tokenized" comprise artwork, gameplay objects, or images and video from a single live broadcast—NBA Top Shots was one of the most popular NFT platforms. According to NFT, the right or licensing rights may or not include the purchase. When you purchase a limited-edition chunk of art, it doesn't mean you own it completely.

As the technology and concept behind NFTs evolve, they may produce a wider variety of works outside the art world.

The blockchain ledger may verify an NFT's unique identity and ownership. Although they were first established on the Ethereum blockchain, they are now accepted on other blockchains such as Flow and Bitcoin Cash. Whether the actual report is a JPEG, audio, GIF, or anything else, the NFT that identifies its owner may be bought and sold just like any other work of art. The price, like genuine art, is largely decided by market demand.

You'd notice a lot of duplicates of great masterpieces if you walked into an art library's gift shop; thus, some NFTs function in the same way. Although certain parts of the chain are entirely genuine, they do not have the same value as the original.

The license for the digital item referred to in NFTs is usually always included, although this does not guarantee copyright ownership. The copyright owner can replicate the work; however, the NFT owner is not compensated.

A school may issue an NFT to students who have finished a degree, letting employers quickly verify an applicant's education. Instead, a venue may use NFTs to acquire and track event tickets, potentially minimizing resale fraud.

7.2 Difference Between Cryptocurrency and NFTs

Cryptocurrencies were designed to act as exchanges by storing quantities or allowing you to purchase and advertise items. Cryptocurrencies, like traditional exchanges like cash, are fungible.

As we've previously explained, a non-fungible token was a certificate of ownership for a digital asset. The asset's worth is determined by its accounts receivable, including its potential future selling value, and NFTs are available for purchase and sale.

Another fantastic example is using art to illustrate the advantages of NFTs.

Depending on your needs, anyone may do it on various platforms to buy NFTs. You'll need a wallet specific to the service you're purchasing from, as well as a coin to put into it. As seen by the landmark sale of Beeple's *Everydays*, NFTs find their way into increasingly popular auction houses.

Because of the high demand for various types of NFT, these are typically distributed in "drops," much as how events are supplied in batches at various times. It indicates that there would be a frantic rush of eager buyers when the drop starts, so be sure to sign up and have your money ready to pay.

7.3 Making Money With Non-Fungible Tokens

NFT is not difficult, and assets are easily accessible to assist decision-making. A specific blockchain is used to create and construct NFTs, with Ethereum NFT being the most popular. In addition to Ethereum, Binance and Flow are often utilized for its expansion. To transact, you'll need to have a crypto wallet and currency, namely Ethereum. Smart contracts may be used to exchange NFTs for cryptocurrency and fiat, with the contract being recorded on a blockchain.

If you've ever wondered how individuals make a livelihood using NFTs, you'll be relieved to learn that there are various options. Take a glance at a little of the many ways that have worked in the past.

Works of Digital Art

Specific NFT artworks are among the most well-known and costly non-fungible tokens constantly manufactured in bank profitability. The story of cryptocurrencies and artwork altered dramatically on March 11, 2021, when an auctioneering firm sold artwork for a whopping 69 million dollars. It was the first time the online auction has sold a digital piece of art. Individual NFT works are among the most well-known and lucrative non-fungible tokens ever generated in income. When artists create digital resources, NFTs provide them the property right, showing proof of uniqueness and profit from their work.

NFTs provide the illustrator with direct ownership of the digital asset, allowing you to demonstrate proof of authenticity and money from your work when you create one. If you become a meme creator, you will profit when your creation gets popular. NFTs seem to be a novel skill for talent makers from that perspective. If you are a numerical art designer, you will have an edge when it is circulated. NFTs are a game-changing tool for art designers when seen in this light.

NFTs in the Fashion Industry

In the same way that artwork addresses authenticity issues and eliminates the possibility of counterfeits, NFTs achieve the same. Apparel and fashion brands are increasingly honoring the NFT curve by creating limited digital publishing of their ensembles, including a selection of iconic celebrity products or design trademarks. Clothing and fashion companies may benefit from NFT education by creating an NFT venue for their clothing and accessories. It allows people to earn unlimited money through NFTs in a safe and secure environment.

Collectibles With a License

Tokenizing collectibles is one of NFTs' most significant targeted functions, and it's also the most natural method to deal with them. People who formerly advertised tangible artifacts such as charms, keepsakes, trade identity cards, and other creatures now just had to promote digital assets. Collectibles may be worth a lot more than their real counterparts, and therefore, NFTs' ability to manufacture rarity is a big plus. So far, baseball cards have become the most popular memorabilia. Initially, the athletic card program only allowed for negotiating registered football player identity cards. The NBA gets its NFT identity card set up. There's a reasonable probability that other sports will stick to the trouser suit, giving hoarders a wider variety of workout NFTs to choose from. It's meant to indicate that the other collectibles aren't doing well.

Computer Games

NFTs for videotape matches are also on the rise because of the blockchain's ability to switch between spending to win and delighting in winning. If you need to draw a bigger audience and increase income potential with higher rewards, you should abandon the NFT match design. Features in the games enable you to purchase, sell, trade, and swap your riches. No applications have gained popular acceptance; nonetheless, the potential is great. On computer-generated goods, tournaments are well-known for having important paymasters. As a result, computer matches including marketable NFTs in large game goods are expected to be a great success. Notably, the producers of NFT audio-visual games are ambitious NFT designers, which may help to propel NFT innovation forward. Unlike other NFTs such as art, vogue, and business postcards, in-competition NFTs appear to be the most advanced of all NFTs. They are smart and responsive, yet they regularly alter as a team's avatar matures and needs to be updated or leveled. Chris Torres, the famous Nyan Cat video creator, created an NFT to sell the animation. Even though Nyan Cat was initially put on the website a decade earlier, Torres decided to auction it off because of the current interest in NFTs. He made a profit of roughly $590,000 using the cryptocurrency Ethereum (ETH). CEO of Twitter Jack Dorsey was among the first NFT transactions to create waves when he sold his first tweet as an NFT. It was finally sold for $2,500,000, and the earnings were donated to charity.

Non-fungible tokens don't seem to be a fad in the blockchain and cryptocurrency worlds. With its many and varied uses, it seems that such knowledge has barely scratched the surface. The fact that only simple explanations are now available demonstrates that no one can precisely forecast cloud computing's full potential.

Like other blockchain experiments, the future of this one is uncertain. According to credible publications, NFTs, do not seem to be fading away anytime soon. They may grow in popularity now that affluent investors are investing in them.

The ability to offer a license to utilize assets without relinquishing control of those assets might be the next huge thing in record sales. Whatever invention you have may be beneficial to join the marketplace to minimize. Game sprites, the music you've recorded, images you've taken, significant accounts on various websites and forums, and quite anything else you can think of are all examples of NFTs.

7.4 The Path to Becoming an NFTs Artist

NFT artists aren't new; the first ones began selling digital art in 2015. After major auctions like Sotheby's did get involved and started selling in the millions of dollars, NFTs became more popular.

Consequently, artists and even alternative movie poster artists have benefitted significantly. Such creators can now sell their digital artwork on the internet without needing an institution to promote them, and they'll be reimbursed for each sale on the private market.

It would be a digital artist specializing in creating digital art and then selling these virtual artworks like non-fungible tokens (NFT).

But precisely, what is a non-fungible token?

NFTs are digital files whose authenticity and provenance may be verified by registering them in a public, computerized, and highly secure database (called a blockchain).

Because the business is always evolving, many blockchains compete for the top place by offering superior NFT solutions. So, the first step is to learn about the many networks and blockchains available and then choose the individual that greatest fits your inspired profile.

SuperRare focuses on digital art, Rarible specializes in digital valuables, and OpeanSea states that CryptoKitties will be its primary emphasis. Consequently, you'll have to choose from the following options: What's your name, by the way? Are you a laid-back illustrator exploring different opportunities? Or are you searching for a fun, current creative that can work with whatever the latest web trend is, no matter how bizarre it may be?

Although some are feasible, some are more popular on specific platforms than others. There is an NFT industry for every digital artist, and non-fungible tokens come in various shapes and sizes. However, those of us on Ethereum's network are the most well-known.

7.5 Choosing the Right Platform

Each website has its registration procedure, with some charging more contract costs than others. You can obtain thorough instructions on becoming a producer on Foundation; you must register to sell products as an NFT on Nifty Gateway. You can join for maybe the first time on KnownOrigin in three different ways.

But don't worry, whatever platform you choose, the process might not be as tricky or terrifying as it seems at this moment. Making NFTs isn't difficult at all.

An NFT may be created from a picture, a video, a comic, a comedy, a label, and any other digital content. After you've chosen your first NFT, then may begin setting up a crypto wallet. You'll be able to manage virtual cash using that wallet, and you'll be listed on NFT markets as well.

Assume you make, buy, and sell art in the actual world with cash.

When creating a crypto wallet, you'll use virtual currency in onli-ne marketplaces to achieve the same. There are various options, like MetaMask, Rainbow, and others. Check that the crypto wa-llets you want to use are compliant with the NFT platform you wish to use.

After you've sorted everything out and made a new bitcoin wallet: Send it some bitcoin. Not all NFTs are compatible with the Ethe-reum platform you have a choice, and if you're fresh to something like this, Ethereum is perhaps the most basic alternative. Because the charge of Ethereum changes so often, it's best to put money into a certain sum rather than acquire a specific quantity of Ethe-reum.

It shouldn't take far more than $200 to create an NFT. As a result, you won't need to make a significant initial expenditure, and it's just for a short time. After choosing your preferred online market, cryptocurrency, and crypto wallet, and after you've received said money in the said wallet, you may create an account on the cho-sen platform. You have had the option of converting your work into an NFT when they join an interactive digital market. NFTs may be readily converted from a popular form like JPG, MP3, or GIF. You may also mention if the NFT is unique or half of a collec-tion and the original price.

Once your NFT artwork has been published as well as minted on the platform, you may start selling it. Others may view it and ma-ybe bid on it; as a result, the initial price may be less than the total price. However, merely placing your work on the internet does not ensure that this will sell. It would help if you sincerely promo-ted yourself or your work. Attend intimate and private Facebook groups and use Twitter and Instagram to hone.

CHAPTER 8

ARE NFTS A GOOD INVESTMENT?

NATHAN REAL

Chapter 8.
ARE NFTS A GOOD INVESTMENT?

In 2021, the popularity of non-fungible tokens, which are unique digital goods like artwork & sports collecting cards validated and maintained via blockchain technology, skyrocketed. People spend millions of dollars creating, collecting, and trading NFTs with the expectation of profiting in the future. On the other hand, experts are doubtful whether NFTs are a worthwhile investment.

Although the boom in NFTs remains relatively fresh, collectors have already traded large sums of money. According to NonFungible, who analyses historical NFT sales data, NFT collectibles have earned over $6.2 billion in revenue since 2017, while digital art has created over $1.9 billion.

According to J. McCormack, a computer science professor at Monash University, "items like artworks and antiques have become the great product of NFTs since they organically fit through what NFTs are. Because digital is easily copied, having this supplementary Certificate of Authentication is critical to demonstrating ownership of that specific item."

Researchers worry that this is not the best moment to join the market, which has grown too large, too quickly, thanks to a lot of excitement and speculation. According to DappRadar, a firm that lets consumers monitor NFTs and other decentralized assets, NFT trade volume increased 38,000% year over year to $10.7 billion in the third quarter.

"This might be the apotheosis, the pinnacle of all bubbles," said Michael Every, Rabobank's Asia-Pacific head of stock market research. "It concerns me much, even though I am completely aware of the dynamics that motivate young people in particular."

Experts say you should acquire an NFT but want to possess it, not just because you want to be part of the craze.

"Don't purchase it because it's an NFT," Vincent co-founder Evan Cohen stated. "Buy it because you appreciate the art, or because you think the item is great, or that you like the community. You would like to be a portion of this in the asset, not just the technology that drives it."

8.1 What Exactly One Receives When They Purchase an NFT?

Because an NFT may only have a single owner at a time, purchasing one grants you exclusive possession of a certain digital object. However, this does not suggest that you have complete authority over who sees or shares that specific piece of art.

Take, for instance, the costliest NFT ever sold: *Everydays: The Very First 5000 Days* is a 5,000-piece digital composite created by Beeple. Vignesh Sundaresan, the originator of both the Metapurse NFT development and Bitaccess, a bitcoin ATM service, is the proprietor of this NFT.

Though Sundaresan is the real owner of just this NFT, millions of others throughout the globe have copied, shared, and watched it—and that's OK! As a result, purchasing an NFT is like buying an autographed print. The NFT is only signed to you, but anybody may look at it. Any digital item may be used as an NFT. So far, they've consisted of:

- Artworks

- Tweets\GIFs

- Purchases made in-game

- Domain names

- Essays

8.2 Why Would Someone Purchase an NFT Token?

You may wonder why anybody would purchase an NFT as you attempt to get your mind all around the strange and mystical world of non-fungible tokens. There are several reasons why folks with extra wealth choose to invest.

Collectability

NFTs are trading papers for the super-rich, like how kids exchange trading cards on the playground. While these cards have no intrinsic value except what the market assigns them, their shifting value makes their collectors' editions and trading potential a high-risk gamble. Consequently, drawing parallels here between NFT as well as the art market is simple. However, unlike the art market, NFTs give artists greater control since they no longer rely on galleries and auction houses to market their work. Artists may sell their artworks immediately to purchasers and retain more revenues by keeping costs low.

8.3 Is It Worthwhile to Put Money into Non-Fungible Tokens?

NFTs attract risk-takers because they offer a one-of-a-kind, high-stakes opportunity to make enormous profits—but be warned, this happens seldom. If you're investigating a more consistent method to invest your money than a Pop-Tart cat GIF, try investing inside an index fund instead. It's not as glamorous, and it has the same cultural cache.

If you want to take a risk and go into the realm of non-fungible tokens, you'll need to create a digital wallet. It is where you'll keep your NFTs and cryptocurrencies. Then you'll need to search for NFTs on sites like OpenSea.io or Rarible, locate one you want, then acquire the appropriate cryptocurrency for that NFT before making your purchase. Then it's just a matter of waiting. You and your Pop-Tart cat have been at the whim of the market since the worth of your NFT is determined by how often someone else is prepared to pay for it.

8.4 How to Purchase NFTs

NFTs are purchased and sold via a dedicated NFT marketplace, like Etsy or Amazon for digital assets. These marketplaces may be used to buy the NFT at a predefined price or even virtual bidding as the trading mechanism for auctioning coins and stocks. Consequently, the prices of NFTs up for auction are volatile, varying in value according to demand. The bigger the market, the higher the price.

Stocks and cryptos are substitutable, implying that one unit is like the others. NFTs, on the other hand, are not. One Amazon share is identical to another, and the Bitcoin token is very similar to another Bitcoin token. NFTs are non-fungible, which means that they permit you to acquire is a one-of-a-kind item that cannot be replaced. You'll need to set up and fund the crypto wallets on an NFT marketplace to trade on these digital assets. Like a wallet app on an e-commerce site, a crypto wallet is where you keep the cryptocurrencies you'll need to buy an NFT. A wallet must be funded only with the coin required to purchase the desired NFT. An NFT developed on the Ethereum blockchain, for example, may need Ether tokens to be bought.

Purchases of NFTs may be made in a variety of marketplaces. Many of the most prominent NFT marketplaces are OpenSea, Foundation, Rarible, and SuperRare. Other specialty markets specialize in certain assets.

8.5 Do You Think NFTs Are a Good Investment for You?

The NFT campaign is very young, but it demonstrates the potential of cryptos to make digitalization operate for a wider range of individuals. For creators, creating and selling digital assets may make a lot of sense. NFTs, on the other hand, are a risky investment whenever it comes to purchasing them. The value of a work is unpredictable and will change depending on demand again for a section.

There's no way to predict which collectibles will flourish and which will not. On the other side, spotting a potential NFT trend might pay out generously in the long term. Some digital works of art sold for cents on the dollar have now sold thousands of dollars. Dabbling in NFT investing may be a good match for you if you like music, collecting art, and other stuff. Consider that item's inventor, the piece's individuality, the asset's possession history, and whether the investment can be used to generate money once purchased when acquiring an asset. In response to the claim that NFTs are indeed a "bubble" ready to burst, bubbles are generally only discovered after the fact. However, keep in mind that digital assets may see a cooling trend in the future. Consider the risks and diversify your holdings by including cryptos and equities of companies developing blockchain technology in your NFT portfolio.

The development of NFTs is still in its early stages. It's a potential new front where technology world but investing in any organization in its infancy comes with many dangers. As you discover more about NFTs, be cautious, and remember to diversify your assets to reduce the chance of a single investment trying to derail your wealth-building efforts.

CHAPTER 9

WHAT IS DECENTRALIZED FINANCE?

NATHAN REAL

Chapter 9.
WHAT IS DECENTRALIZED FINANCE?

9.1 DeFi

The decentralized finance, or DeFi, was coined in a Telegram conversation in 2018. Major software engineers and businesspeople struggled to develop a name for their concept of computerized, blockchain-based payment institutions' potential of displacing traditional banks. DeFi has increased in reputation over the last three years. A crypto wallet allows a user to exchange digital assets, obtain loans, and buy insurance, amongst many other things. And over 10 million subscribers have installed MetaMask, among the most prominent mobile currencies used to access these systems, which has almost 100 billion dollars in assets. The foundations of decentralized finance can be traced back to the 2008 bitcoin paper, which laid the groundwork for a unique digital currency system; a few years ago, Ethereum was born. In her article, *The Endless Machine*, Camila Rosso, creator of the crypto news service The Defiant, writes, "Bitcoin wants to be peer-to-peer money. Ethereum intended to be everything consensus." DeFi is a combination of encryption, finance, and project management, and it has its language and terminology. Let's break it down into manageable chunks.

Decentralization

Decentralized finance is characterized by the truth that it is decentralized. Consider, for instance, bitcoin: The initial crypto asset is essentially a decentralized record (the blockchain), with events data from databases on many different computers. Encryption is used to safeguard that single record, and the computers keep track of each other to ensure it hasn't been tampered with. Similarly, even if a state tries to stop multiple computers or another network from supporting bitcoin, the digital asset may continue to operate because other computers on the network keep complete track of data and can continue to operate the game. This notion is taken a step further with DeFi. Blockchains, such as the Ethereum platform, which Indian developer Vitalik Buterin suggested in 2013, are used in decentralized exchanges and lending systems. Unlike the bitcoin network, which was established to log financial transactions, Bitcoin and Ethereum cryptocurrency was meant to host applications. Consider Ethereum as a decentralized computer for which software developers may create decentralized apps (dApps). Ethereum's processing speed is compensated in Ether, the foremost valued cryptocurrency behind bitcoin. The Ethereum network, like Bitcoin, is difficult to close or manipulate, and it is accessible to everyone with a connection to the internet.

Governance

DeFi companies' judgment, or democracy, is frequently decentralized, from the rates they charge customers to the goods they supply. (Think of DeFi as a true democracy, but the US system of government is a democratic republic.) A decentralized program may be driven by a single person or a small number of individuals at first. Still, as the project gathers traction, they frequently seek to step back and transfer it to the community that uses it. This shift might take the shape of a decentralized autonomous organization (DAO) that has its laws and regulations written in computer software and may issue democracy tokens, allowing currency holders to vote in choices.

Peer to Peer

The ability for multiple individuals to conduct digital payments directly to each other was one of bitcoin's fundamental advances. Using sheet or metal currency is simple to do in the material realm. However, before Bitcoin, the only method to do so electronically was via banks or a payment system like eBay. Going via these third parties creates a digital trace that may be tracked, but those firms might be "censored" by the government, meaning they could be forced to block transactions for political or other reasons. Bitcoin was created to solve this problem by serving as a digital currency for peer-to-peer transactions. Mentoring DeFi applications are also possible. A trade is routed via several intermediaries in normal stock activity, including dealers and exchangers. At the same time, the assets are kept at a custody bank, which is responsible for preventing the securities from being lost or stolen. A DeFi market, on the other hand, does not have such middlemen. Suppose you transfer cryptocurrency units on Uniswap, a decentralized exchange based on the Ethereum network. In that case, those assets will wind up in your crypto wallet thanks to Uniswap's automatic programs referred to as smart agreements. As a result, fewer parties will take a percentage of your sale.

ICOs and NFTs

Since its inception 13 years ago, Bitcoin has permitted a succession of electronic cash rushes. Cryptocurrency launches (ICOs) and non-fungible tokens (NFTs) were two of people: A sort of crowdsourcing, initial coin offerings (ICOs) are frequently used to collect funds for open systems initiatives. ICO investors receive a one-of-a-kind token in return for their money, which may or may not grant them entry to the computer's unique characteristics or nothing at all. ICOs can sound an awful lot like a share sale, much like a stock offering for the US Financial Services Authority; coin offers may not have the same safeguards as a controlled stock economy's going public (IPO), such as transparency and monitoring. So, according to CB Insights, ICOs generated more than $7 billion in 2018 before plummeting by over 95% to $371.000 in 2019, the most recent year for which data is accessible, as regulators clamped down. NFTs are like restricted collectibles, but they're only available online. Blockchain technology allows people to create unique digital goods such as antiques and art, just as it enables users to establish ownership of their Bitcoin holdings. Unlike MP3s, which can be copied and pasted indefinitely, NFTs are intended to be unique and only have one owner at a time. Andrew Warhol and Michael Winkelmann's paintings are displayed at a contemporary art fair in Hong Kong.

How Does Decentralized Finance Work?

DeFi, instead of an institution, employs technology to facilitate payments and operations among participants. Along with public blockchains, various tries to reach are being created, establishing a foundation for decentralized money to function on. A monetary system requires two primary elements to function: a network and money. Banking institutions serve as the infrastructure under a centralized system, whereas a monetary system, such as the US dollar, serves as the currency. Decentral finance should substitute these elements to provide a comprehensive range of financial services.

Infrastructure

Ethereum is a decentralized program writing environment. We can develop smart contracts computerized software that could be used to handle banking services—using Ethereum. You can create rules for how a commercial bank will operate using contracts and then deploy these principles on Ethereum. A private blockchain can't be changed after it's been deployed. On Ethereum, users may create decentralized apps to create any banking product, and agreements can operate such services independently.

Currency

You'll need to have a strong currency to build trustworthy, secure decentralized finances. The Ethereum infrastructure is incompatible with blockchain, and Ether, Ethereum's customizable coinage, is extremely volatile. A virtual currency is a virtual currency with a fiat that maintains its worth. DAI is a decentralized stable coin tied to the US dollar, which means that 1 DAI is worth 1 dollar. DAI's worth is secured by cryptocurrency collateral instead of guaranteed solely by US currency reserves. DAI is the best money for decentralized commerce for its reliability.

Decentralized Financial Services

Beyond online payments, the advantages of a decentralized finance system are numerous. Money transfer is only one part of the existing centralized financial system; however, decentralized finance aims to replace all system components, including markets, loans, insurers, and savings accounts. On Ethereum, blockchain networks enable these decentralized services to exist and run fairly and safely. The following are some of the financial products that Ethereum currently supports:

Decentralized Borrowing and Lending

You may get a credit in a short amount of time, thanks to decentralized financing, without bothering to go through the lengthy or restrictive application procedure. The Compound is a decentralized, peer-to-peer lending and borrowing service built on Ethereum. The Compound links lenders electronically and administers loans autonomously via smart contracts. As a result, the practice of "yield farming" has grown in popularity, as anybody may provide their crypto assets and gain relevance in the method. The Compound may also deposit Bitcoin as protection and loan national currencies against that.

Decentralized Exchange

The cryptocurrency exchange (DEX) enables us to purchase, sell, or trade coins on the Ethereum network without going via an exchange operator, without requiring sign-ups or ID verification, but without incurring any withdrawal fees. Additionally, unlike centralized exchanges, exchanging using DEX does not require an upfront deposit. Contracts govern the conditions and procedure of trades, which are implemented independently.

Decentralized Insurance

Friend, decentralized insurance is also possible thanks to smart contracts in the decentralized financial system. In a decentralized financial sector, you may interact with anybody in the world wanting to cover your possessions. You can guarantee other people's money for a fee, often without going to an insurance broker or agent. All occur independently, with financial intermediaries assuring that the process is fair, safe, and reliable.

9.2 Advantages and Disadvantages

Devolution makes DeFi harder to control or eradicate, but it needs a lot of processing power. Keeping a database and information over a network of numerous machines slows down transactions and can increase transaction costs. The most prominent blockchain for DeFi apps is Ethereum. However, the massive processing quantity is currently pushing up costs and slowing down the network. Other chains like Solana and Avalanche are gaining traction as Ethereum developers strive to figure out how to make it more scalable. "It's very difficult to get speed out of blockchain systems," says Emin Gün Sirer, a Cornell University software engineer and Avalanche adviser. DeFi eliminates middlemen such as custodial banks, which seem to keep assets (typically digital tokens) secure. That means you won't have to worry about just a commercial bank going bankrupt and stealing your assets with it, but about the government controlling and collecting your assets. On either side, you and your password are the only ones who can keep your assets safe. If you forget (or someone steals), all your valuables are lost forever. The DeFi innovators frequently claim to be open to everybody. Without typical financial credentials like identity or a credit score, you might be able to secure a loan or trade virtual currency. That liberty has the potential to bring financial services to parts of the nation that haven't previously had such or where they are too expensive or vulnerable to fraud or seizure. However, the disadvantage is obvious: thieves might use the systems or run contrary to government regulations if no one notes who is utilizing a service or where they are situated. The attack on regulations has already started. While blockchains have proven difficult to break, the smart contracts and apps that operate on top of them are only as intelligent as those who created them. Its code is generally open, which implies it's available for everyone to examine and modify, making it more vulnerable to hackers. The far more actual coding is audited for security flaws these days. An increasing number of individuals know the significance of formal verification (a method that involves algorithms to analyze other algorithms for flaws). However, according to Cornell's Sirer, a bunch of cash continues into code that has not been spruced up as an adult.

9.3 DeFi Apps

Three dApps you should know about:

Uniswap

Hayden Adams, a materials scientist from New York, founded Uniswap, a decentralized exchange (DEX). The concept came from Ethereum co-founder Buterin's blog articles about creating an autonomous broker-dealer and decentralized exchange. According to CoinGecko, a crypto-data website, Uniswap now enables $1 billion each in daily crypto trade, and its administration tokens, UNI, have a market price of roughly $36 million.

AAVE

Stand Kulechov, a law student, launched Aave in 2017. (Originally called ETHLend). The system allows people to give and borrow crypto tokens; Defi Pulse said individuals had put up nearly $14 billion in security to repay the ecosystem.

MakerDAO

MakerDAO is the main refinancing framework built on the Dai stablecoin, pegged to the US dollar. MakerDAO was formed in 2014, with Rune Christensen as a co-founder. MakerDao claims to be one of the largest decentralized apps on the Ethereum blockchain and the first DeFi software to gain widespread popularity on its homepage. On the platform, users had put up around $6 billion in collateral.

9.4 Errors and Hacking

In DeFi, programming faults and workarounds are widespread. Because bitcoin events are irrevocable, an inaccurate or fraudulent payment on a DeFi network is difficult to undo. Yam Finance, a company that unveiled in 2020, swiftly raised its funds to $750 million before failing due to a technical issue a few days later. Furthermore, the cryptographic protocol technology that implements DeFi platforms often offers a set that can be created automatically to build up rival platforms, causing instability as funds transfer from desktop to mobile. The group or individual behind a DeFi technology may be unidentified, and clients' funds may be lost. Some DeFi methods have been labeled "Ponzi-like" by entrepreneur Michael Novogratz.

DeFi has been linked to the excitement of the 2017 bitcoin tech bubble initial coin offering (ICO). Owing to the intelligence necessary to connect with DeFi platforms and the lack of a middleman with client staff, novice traders are at a higher risk of financial loss. While cryptocurrency-related crime (including ransomware) has decreased dramatically since its peak in 2019, DeFi-related criminality has surged appreciably. DeFi was accountable for an additional part of bitcoin crime in 2021. This increase has been linked to a mix of builder ineptitude and either non-existent or badly implemented restrictions. Outside hackers robbing from susceptible DeFi initiatives or "rug tugs," when developers and pundits push a company and then leave with the currency as a type of pump-and-dump, are two examples of DeFi robbery.

CHAPTER 10

NFT AND ENVIRONMENT

NATHAN REAL

Chapter 10.
NFT AND ENVIRONMENT

NFTs are one-of-a-kind digital tokens that grant someone ownership of a work of art, such as a film, song, or photograph, through a wide variety of computer transactions. Traditional cryptocurrencies, such as Bitcoin, are interchangeable. NFTs, on other hand, are one-of-a-kind digital works of art. (It's like how you can easily exchange a $20 bill with 2 bills of $10 but not a Picasso for just a Monet.) The market for purchasing and selling NFTs is growing at a breakneck pace because of COVID-19. As a result of the pandemic, "because we're living electronically more than ever before," said Aubrey Strobel, communications director for Lolli, an even more Bitcoin rewards application. "The pandemic has increased the digital period users spend online, making digitally native business owners like NFTs more appealing," he added in an interview with Bankrate. There's a lot of cash on the table. And the world of non-virtual art is taking notice. Artists are creating NFTs with a track record of work, and prominent art auction houses like Christie's organize sales. NFTs appear to be a growing part of the art scene in the 21 century.

Climatological activist J. Lemercier, a French artist well renowned for his perspective light sculptures, made the transition from artist to climate activist 2 years ago. He has participated in anti-coal mining demonstrations. He has projected lasers over excavators and government buildings to spectacular effect and has launched a campaign asking that Autodesk cease providing its design tools to fossil fuel companies. It included a substantial heating cost for his studio in Brussels, power again for high-end computers that he uses to produce his masterpieces, even hundreds of flights every year to present his work at various venues throughout the globe. He measured everything down to a watt and committed to minimizing his energy consumption by 10% every year, a target he had already achieved. For many months, he made significant progress, but growth was undone entirely in a couple of moments a few months earlier. The issue began with Lemercier's first blockchain "drop," which was the genesis of the problem. The purchase of 6 as such non-fungible tokens, aka NFTs, was part of the event, which came in the form of short movies inspired by the notion of platonic solids and distributed to attendees. Lemercier's works in the real world, which feature black metal polyhedrons that circle on a loop and glitter, are mentioned in the film, as are his projects in the virtual world. After being put up for sale on a site named Nifty Gateway, the artworks were up for auction and sold out in less than 1 minute for 6 figures. According to information he subsequently obtained from Crypto Art, the sale also burned 8.7 megawatt-hours of electricity. That amount equated to 2 years' worth of power use in Lemercier's studio space. The artwork has been resold during the intervening year, resulting in an additional year's worth of effort. There was still more money to be gained. As far as Lemercier was concerned, the issue extended well beyond himself. Even as the crypto art world grew, he watched his fellow artists become billionaires almost overnight. However, their contribution to carbon emissions was also significant. Artists didn't seem to comprehend the scale of the problem—including Lemercier himself—and the platforms facilitating the sales didn't appear interested in providing clarification.

10.1 Environmental Impact

NFTs and their cryptocurrency counterparts have one thing in common: they both consume a lot of energy. Bitcoin mining already emits 38 million tons of CO_2 annually, more than Slovakia's carbon footprint. According to a 2018 study today in Nature Climate Change, Bitcoin emissions alone may boost Earth's temperature by 2 degrees.

"Bitcoin is a solid evidence blockchain, which means it secures the blockchain and verifies transactions using proof-of-work (PoW) consensus procedures." According to S. Köhler, a Ph.D. student & sustainable blockchain tech expert at Aalborg University of Denmark, "PoW means all miners compete against to mine a block. To win in these challenges, specialized computers create trillions of guesses every second. It's what you'd call a "brute-force" approach, and this is what necessitates a significant amount of electricity."

In context, Bitcoin's daily carbon footprint is akin to watching 1.3 million hours on YouTube videos. It also utilizes the same amount of electricity daily that an ordinary American household does on the period of 25 days. NFTs have a similar environmental impact because they require energy-intensive computing transactions to validate and sell the art.

"To produce NFTs, to auction, to pay again for NFT after purchasing the property, or to transfer ownership," Köhler explains, "transactions on a blockchain are required. So, you might link the number of transactions NFTs require to the amount of electricity they consume, as well as their environmental imprint. The connected impact of NFTs grows as interest in them grows, and more individuals buy and sell them."

Because miners are obliged to utilize low-cost power to maximize earnings, Köhler believes energy consumption during these exchanges is a concern (like fossil fuels). Additionally, she discusses the technologies employed: "The manufacturing and repurposing of the hardware is a minor portion of the total," she explains. The use of specialized computers in mining that might become unprofitable in a few years generates significant volumes of e-waste, as previously stated.

10.2 Eco-Friendly Alteration

Now, the crypto-world is attempting to alter its course. Many platforms are increasingly promoting their environmental sensitivity. Processes like those used at the Canadian facility, which uses a Currency Works protocol known as Zer00, are gaining popularity. Fortunately, advancements in cryptocurrency storing information provide appealing options. The actual sites in which some organizations mine coins are even pickier, with some corporations searching for spots that employ renewable energy sources or have additional energy on hand. Renewable energy sources account for around 39% of bitcoin mining currently in use. However, cryptocurrency is still in its infancy, and each month brings with it new efficiencies. In reaction to the rapid shift, they have witnessed in their profession, Israeli engineers Eli Ben-Sassoon and Uri Kolodny founded StarkWare. The Baby Boomers occupy this area, rather than the software developers and Gen Z artists who've been more often in the news. The two have theoretical and intellectual backgrounds, respectively. One of many teams has created a method of reducing the carbon footprint of Ethereum mining and transactions by compressing more information through each block of a blockchain, which is currently under development. (Brands seeking to enter the NFT space, such as Marvel and Disney, have already done sign up to employ StarkWare's tech in their NFT launch because Ethereum is presently the leading cryptocurrency in terms of the trading volume. In addition, they just completed a $50 m Series C fundraising round into a $2 billion value. According to the company, this technique may cut energy usage by anywhere from 200–200,000 times compared to previous solutions, but the figure is almost endless strictly theoretical. According to Ben-Sasson, "If you think of each block of a bitcoin as something that emits a lot of carbon dioxide from all the mining activity that takes place, there are fixed expenses that are very, extremely high." he adds. "Consider it as if it were an aircraft that throws out a large amount of carbon." When you can put 600,000 people on an aircraft instead of 100 people, even if the flight emits the very same amount of carbon dioxide as before—which is terrible—the impact on the environment is rather good in terms of a footprint per person. It is precisely at this point that we come in."

NFTs can now be packed onto a single block of silicon, according to Kolodny, thanks to the company's new technology. StarkWare has developed a tool known as a ZK rollup, which stands for "zero-knowledge" rollup, that allows transactions off-chain, reducing energy consumption. Whether or not new chains that are just not "proof of work" and different rollups like StarkWare's can—or would—then reasonably options to the core "work" of bitcoin is currently one of the essential heated discussions in the blockchain world. While the most prominent crypto platforms, like Bitcoin and Ethereum, continue to use "proof of work," other rivals, including Solana, Binance, Flow, and Tezos, use "proof of stake," which consumes less energy, thus, being more efficient. StarkWare is such an example of a firm that provides a mechanism to make Ethereum payments more efficient; the company is remarkable for the high-profile clientele that it has signed up with.

10.3 Greener, Leaner NFTs?

People attempt to iron out the wrinkles in all the offered remedies as the climate issue worsens daily. Some individuals will continue to refuse to engage in a system that they believe is intrinsically bad and ecologically damaging, even against the authentic background of climate-related tragedies. When you visit cryptoart. wtf, you'll see a notice directing you to several GitHub sites and articles that walk you through carbon footprint estimates and current thinking on the subject. "CryptoArt contributes just a small portion of world emissions," the letter states. "We believe that our activities in this place reflect an attitude that we must have to effect systemic change on a bigger scale." All the possible solutions to a climate pollution issue posed by NFTs are now being researched and developed to varying degrees, even though they have still not been widely adopted. Many artists—and some environmentalists—are enthusiastic about the future of cryptographic art. "I suppose that within the following year or year and a half, emissions will be a non-issue," said Pallant of the Blockchain for Climate Foundation.

Performers are the most vocal about the need for change. If the markets for NFTs do not begin to match their needs, artists may resort to minting their own NFTs on marketplaces utilizing more environmentally friendly cryptocurrencies. An artist-led movement is gathering funds to reward those developing innovative approaches to make cryptographic art more financially viable. Individuals who want to support such artists by purchasing their work may migrate alongside them towards less damaging platforms or purchase a tangible copy of the work.

10.4 Assembling Energy Use

Lemercier was aware that energy is involved in anything related to the blockchain. However, he was unaware of the implications of distributing a collection of artworks and had difficulty locating information. It couldn't possibly be that much money, and he reasoned, particularly when compared to his regular operation of making and distributing tangible items. Furthermore, the possibilities were enticing. He preferred the new form of ownership compared to established art markets since it seemed to impose fewer restrictions on up-and-coming artists. Therefore, Lemercier agreed: since heating was the most expensive energy source in his studio, he agreed to spend a percentage of the cryptocurrency revenues on improved insulation. Memo Akten, a friend & fellow technological artist, became aware of the project and expressed worry about his environmentally sensitive buddy being engaged in blockchain technology. Did Lemercier truly understand the full scope of the environmental costs? Following the blockchain activity related to 18,000 NFT artworks, Akten decided to track it. He discovered that power use was more involved than just adding one token to a blockchain. Another transaction to consider was the hundreds of bids that artwork may get, as well as resales in the fast-moving non-fungible token market.

Furthermore, some artists published many "editions" of their works, increasing the energy used further. Lemercier has published 6 NFTs, yet 53 editions of his books. Akten was inspired to develop Cryptoart because of this revelation. WTF is a type of roulette game in which a piece of crypto art is chosen, and an approximate estimate of energy consumption and emissions is shown. The goal of the website, according to Akten, is not to embarrass musicians but rather to embarrass the platforms that monitor the sales. According to him and Lemercier, the goal is for the NFT markets to embrace more sophisticated equipment tools that manage more parts of transactions besides the blockchain or abandon Ethereum in favor of alternative blockchains that do not need mining.

J. Crain, the CEO for SuperRare, a prominent non-fungible tokens marketplace, believes it is incorrect to correlate blockchain transactions with carbon footprint and that the website sensationalizes the problem by attempting to assign a particular energy usage figure number to a piece of artwork. He says the cryptocurrency is analogous to an aircraft that will take off independent of how many crypto-artists join the plane. Consequently, it is unfair to artists to claim that they are responsible for the CO_2 emissions. "There is an entire ecosystem of individuals who are making emissions," he argues. In addition, what about the greenhouse gas emissions involved with the conventional, tangible art world? Every feature has been painstakingly planned, from the plane trips and crate shipment of artworks to the gallery lighting and security systems.

"I share the greater worries about emissions," Crain adds, particularly even as the blockchain art industry increases in popularity. To make the transactions increasingly efficient, SuperRare is looking at many solutions, he adds, albeit many of them entail trade-offs in terms of security. He claims that the controversy has heightened his enthusiasm for Ethereum 2.0. Artists like Akten & Lemercier have expressed their dissatisfaction with the reception, which has not diminished. As Akten explains, "they believe that the problem will be resolved in the next year or two. Therefore, it's OK to be predatory right now." As for carbon emissions linked with the conventional art world, the question is why they aren't at the pinnacle of the agendas since the goal of blockchain artwork is to conceive something completely new. "We have to modify our established patterns," Akten asserts emphatically. "But how can we create new networks that are unsustainable?"

After hearing about his carbon impact, Lemercier canceled 2 scheduled drops that had been initially priced at $200,000 each. He admits that he understands why artists choose to continue their work. According to him, "I can see why kids want to ride the wave since it has the potential to set them up for life." However, he has been looking for options in recent months. He had tried out a sale on a site that was already proof-of-stake, and everything had gone well for him. It didn't have the same number of artists and consumers, but he was curious whether he might persuade many artists to move to generate interest. Perhaps a well-known musician will cancel a significant Ethereum fall in solidarity with them to show their support.

Meanwhile, Lemercier was pleased to be re-entering the actual art scene, which was becoming more straightforward as the pandemic limitations were relaxed a little more each day. He had just presented a solo exhibition of his work in Madrid, and he took a train to get there.

10.5 Million-Dollar Sales

Massive sales of crypto art, also known as NFT art (a non-fungible form of art)—the field's practitioners haven't yet agreed on the terminology—are now taking place, garnering widespread attention. An animated picture of Nyan Cat, the iconic meme depicting a rainbow-shooting kitty formed from a Pop-Tart, was acquired for $660,000 inside a blockchain auction last month, according to CoinDesk. Beeple, an artist noted for his humorously grotesque views on current events and who has an ongoing sale at Christie's, has received a $3.5 million offer in an ongoing auction at Christie's for an NFT. The above, however, is only the tip of an exciting industry. A thriving genre among TikTok videos advises viewers on rapidly flip pieces by lesser-known artists for a tidy profit and works by fewer artists often sell worth thousands of dollars. No one can make sense of the figures, and the same can be stated of some artwork sent to the auction block. However, this was also true lately for the values of GameStop stocks and Dogecoin, among other things. For digital speculators, it's a weird and intoxicating moment to be alive. The appeal of blockchain technology for digital artists is that it provides a new paradigm of ownership. It is no safer copycats than any other material on the web; a person may capture a screenshot or video a picture and proudly show the duplicate on the computer's screen.

In contrast, with just an NFT, each owner purchases a confirmed token that serves as digital proof that the artwork is theirs—like an artist's signature. The objective is to provide a sense of the legitimacy of natural art to encourage people to buy it. After all, most people would agree that an excellent replica of a Mondrian abstraction painted on your door frame is not anything like the original made by the painter. It's hard to see why the same couldn't be said for a.CAS file. As an added plus, the concept allows for ownership of the token to be expanded to resales, enabling artists to continue to get a portion of the proceeds. However, it is necessary to acknowledge that this approach uses a significant amount of energy. Ethereum is used by the largest markets for NFT art, including Nifty Gateway, MakersPlace, and SuperRare, to conduct their sales. Ethereum is responsible for maintaining a secure ledger of cryptocurrencies and NFT transactions, which is done via a process referred to as mining. Like the system that validates Bitcoin transactions, the system involves a computer network that utilizes sophisticated encryption to determine whether exchanges are legitimate in doing so, consumes energy on the size of a small nation—and requires energy just on the size of such a small country. The precise nature of how energy consumption translates into carbon emissions is indeed a widely debated topic. According to some estimations, 70% of mining activities may be fuelled by environmentally friendly sources. However, that figure varies seasonally, and with a global energy system powered mainly by fossil fuels, detractors argue that energy consumption is just energy consumption. Existing activities in certain mining hotspots, such as Montana and Missoula, which have benefited from cheap hydropower, have been prohibited because of fears that even "clean" mining may force adjacent energy consumers to utilize dirtier energy sources. However, there is no definite timetable for the relocation ever since it has been in the runs for some years.

You should first identify what digital content asset you wish to portray in an NFT before you can generate one. Following that, the property must be minted. It entails securing the token produced on the blockchain using a cryptographic key. Simply put, a unique key is created and recorded on the ledger to show the asset. Ethereum is a highly applied cryptocurrency for NFTs. For example, the "digital content property," a video snippet, is usually kept in a different location (known as "off-chain" storage). The cryptographic key is programmed to include asset information (metadata), check if a related file is legitimate (with links), validate the holder's identity, and are also designed to include typical decentralized applications as stored in the system.

CHAPTER 11

FAQS

NATHAN REAL

Chapter 11.
FAQS

Stephen Curry, the champion of the NBA, eventually paid around USD 180,000 for an Ape Yacht Club NFT, which now has sparked a lot of debate and skepticism about NFTs. NFT market price quadrupled in 2020, hitting over $250 million, and NFT sales topped $2 billion throughout the initial phase of the year 2021, even though the innovation has been there since 2014. Here are the most common questions that investors have concerning NFTs.

11.1 What Is an NFT?

Non-fungible tokens, or NFTs, are cryptographic commodities on the blockchain that include unique identifier codes and information that differentiate them from one another. NFTs are one-of-a-kind and not replaceable, which implies no two are alike. NFTs could be anything from a one-of-a-kind digital artwork to a limited-edition shoe, in-game item, or digital collectible. Non-fungible tokens, or NFTs, are cryptographically safe data units that certify a digital asset's legitimacy and ownership. A cryptocurrency is used to secure the NFT. It implies that the asset's and its owner's information is stored on a public ledger. When you publish on a distributed network rather than a central hub, you don't have a particular document of possession; instead, you have a synchronized database across multiple nodes. All participants observe each transaction. As a result, various systems verify all ownership and changes of ownership. As a result, distributed ledgers provide built-in security against counterfeiting, corruption, and cyber-attacks that traditional ledger systems lack.

Furthermore, the evidence of ownership is unchangeable. The non-fungibility of an NFT is one of its most important characteristics. Fungibility refers to reciprocal interchangeability; for example, a £10 bill may be exchanged for 2 £5 bills, 10 £1 coins, 20 50-pence pieces, or any other combination of the currency—the units of the product are comparable and indistinguishable. Bitcoin is an example of a fungible crypto asset or crypto-token. NFTs, on the other hand, are non-fungible, which implies they can't be divided or replaced. Each NFT is one-of-a-kind (unlike £1 coins or other fungible assets).

11.2 What Makes an NFT Valuable?

The worth of an NFT is determined by the asset it symbolizes, which is typically something electronic, such as an original work of art or digital artifacts. The virtual asset is not necessarily contained in the NFT, but it refers to its blockchain presence. An NFT, like something of a performance pass or a deed to real estate, reflects the worth of the object it symbolizes.

11.3 How Do NFTs Work?

Paintings and other conventional art pieces are expensive since they are a thing. Digital files, on the other hand, may be indefinitely reproduced. Artwork may be "tokenized" with NFTs to generate a digital proof of purchase that can be purchased and sold. A track of who has what, similar to crypto-currency, is kept on a public ledger blockchain network. Since the ledger is kept by mul-

tiple computers all over the globe, the data could be fabricated. NFTs can also include decentralized applications that, for instance, offer the artist a percentage of any subsequent token sales.

11.4 What's the Connection Between NFTs and Cryptocurrency?

NFTs are not cryptocurrencies, and they are based on Ethereum and Bitcoin-like technologies. In addition, NFTs, like cryptocurrencies, are stored on a network, which confirms their unique identification and ownership. In addition, the blockchain maintains track of all transactions involving the NFT and the property it symbolizes. The Ethereum platform is home to a large number of NFTs.

11.5 How to Make an NFT?

Anyone may make an NFT. All you'll need now is mobile payment, buy a little Ethereum, and access to an NFT platform in which you can publish and convert your work into an NFT or crypto artworks.

11.6 How to Buy NFT and Sell NFT?

NFTs are often purchased via a variety of curated technology platform sites. NFTs are commonly purchased and traded on open marketplaces like OpenSea.io. SuperRare, MakersPlace, Nifty Gateway, Rarible, and KnownOrigin are all good places to go for digital painting. Some sites, such as OpenSea, take both USD and crypto, while others solely accept bitcoin…

11.7 How to Know if NFT Is Authentic and How Is an NFT Valued? What Are the Most Expensive NFTs?

The blockchain records NFT possession, and that transaction serves as a digital pink slip. The price of an NFT varies greatly depending on the technology innovation being traded. Because NFTs have become a more popular means to buy and sell digital art, evaluating an NFT would consider an author's reputation and previous NFT transactions. At 600 ETH, Dragon the CryptoKitty remains among the most expensive NFTs in space.

11.8 Will NFTs Be the Hope of Graphic Arts and Collectible Things, and Can NFTs Be Used as an Investment?

What you ask is a factor. NFTs appeal to artists, singers, sports, celebrities, and others because they provide a fresh and different way to sell their commodities directly to followers, including GIFs, memes, and tweets. If the NFT is sold to a new owner, artists can program ongoing royalties, and galleries view a new generation of collectors as a possible target. NFTs can be utilized as an investment in the current circumstances, and an NFT can be purchased and profitably resold. Some NFT markets also allow NFT sellers to get royalties for the assets they sell.

11.9 How Are NFTs Purchased and Traded?

After the NFT has been created, the inventor can sell it on an NFT market such as OpenSea or Rarible. Many NFT producers have established their marketplaces, and an advertising campaign will be conducted. Anyone intrigued in the NFT will enter the market when it goes live and put bids with their on-marketplace purse, which may store cryptocurrency, including things such as Ethereum or fiat cash. The winning bidder's cash will be exchanged, and the NFT will be sent to their light of the fact account. NFTs can be traded in private markets offered by NFT platforms or by making sales to a buyer's lateral wallet transfers. All activities are added to the blockchain, and since it is an immutable network, all ledger members are "observed" to each event. There is a complete record of possession in this manner.

11.10 What Can NFTs Be Used For?

NFTs have become incredibly common and have a variety of applications because of their resistance to manipulation, the gua-rantee of validity and control, and non-fungibility. The artistic, sports, and academic sectors are the primary users of NFTs and their grounds data. They are being used by sports organizations, teams, organizations, and athletes to monetize digital athlete photographs, digital memorabilia, and films of iconic athletic mo-ments, among other things. The NBA's Top Shots platform has produced over $700 million in revenue. So rare, an NFT virtual sporting event with license deals with various football national associations, teams, and high-profile players, are two examples of great successes. These platforms and their customers can con-tinue to benefit over the period through charges and royalty whi-le still maintaining some authority by permitting "selling" and resellers. Video games and shrewd tickets have been made with

NFTs, nothing other than digitalized tickets. Real Madrid uses NFT intelligent passes to deliver special benefits to fans who visit or watch a game. Kings of Leon issued an NFT edition of their record that included "gold stars" that could be used to get assured front-line VIP seating at one of the shows. Certain designers have utilized NFTs and blockchain-based stuff to create video games, mostly based on gathering up markets.

Axie Infinity is a computer game built on NFTs inside which users buy and exchange comic monster NFTs. Each has its unique qualities and "powers." Afterward, they employ these NFT creatures in combat against those other players. Axie Infinity's company stock worth is $3.2 million, with shares outstanding worth $1 trillion. Emojibles is a computer game where users purchase, trade, and fight Emoji NFTs. Grimes and Steve Aoki have utilized NFTs to release music videos and tracks previously unavailable on other platforms. NFT sets have also been "dropped" by Damien Hirst and Andy Warhol. Many musicians have said that adopting NFTs has saved them money by eliminating intermediaries.

Furthermore, musicians have begun to employ NFTs to benefit from increased resale royalty following well-publicized complaints of low royalty platforms. Many films and television series are also expected to be released as NFTs. In addition, Twitter's 1st Tweet was transformed into an NFT. Because NFTs utilize smart contracts in their programming (many of which follow Ethereum specifications, the code may incorporate connections to documents (such as other pacts), demand proof of identification, and certify document validity which is important where counterparties are needed.

11.11 What Are the Economics?

NFT markets, in principle, provide such a venue for painters and content owners to distribute their work messages to specific consumers who are NFT community users through all the selling of

NFTs that validate digital art and collectibles. In addition to cost savings, the inventor and software engineers and the auction platform will partake in the first auction price. On successive transactions of the NFT, the developer, development team, and maybe the platform might profit from the direct sale. It is also necessary to integrate NFTs with threshold selling prices, or even peak sale prices, to control the secondary market for the individual NFT. Depending on the creator's intentions, personal brand, and other factors, this may be needed to preserve a degree of prestige and promote, or prevent, regular trading or prediction on the NFT.

11.12 What Do I Own in an NFT?

When people acquire an NFT, the amount of their possession is determined by the NFTs blockchain network or the marketplace's or author's clauses. As a result, designers have a lot of leeways. Investors will possess the NFT on the bitcoin and the digital currency at a minimum, but this does not imply ownership of the fundamental copyrights or any copyrights. Observe how, when a person purchases a painting, they do not instantly get the right to replicate and sell the portrait for their creation since the artist retains the property. Kings of Leon made their NFT records available primarily for personal use, preventing any financial use. In certain situations, developers will enable their NFT to be used financially, but only under the terms of a non-exclusive, semi-license. For instance, the clauses of CryptoKitties allow the purchaser to commercialize their CryptoKitty for up to $100,000 total salary per year, including through retailing. Many NFT agreements also include code that enables the initial developer to partake in income and collect royalties from the selling and usage of NFTs. Likewise, founders who own copyrights in their NFTs subject matter should think around whether one's possess privileges are fully protected but whether a permit or allocation of rights relating to the artistic and innovative subject matter, including the underpinning job and code, is suitable. Legal guidance should be obtained to guarantee that intellectual property is appropriately used and preserved.

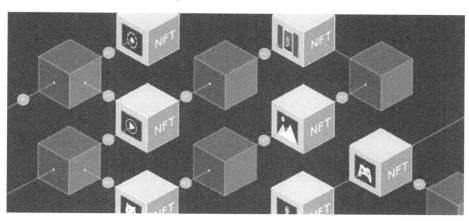

11.13 Are NFTs Here to Stay?

Even though no technology's long-term performance can be assured, NFTs' immensely adaptable nature ensures that they will continue to thrive. The software system gives immutable evidence of property, non-fungibility validates individuality, and decentralized technology assures security and protection. More sectors will utilize NFTs and Ethereum blockchain as the industry evolves..

CONCLUSION

NATHAN REAL

Conclusion

There's no longer any justification for not investing in NFTs; there's no great moment than now. Whether a complete beginner or an experienced veteran, this guide will help you achieve a prosperous start as a starting NFTs investor. The devoted reader will go on an educational journey that starts with conventional finance and continues with crypto assets, decentralized finance, non-fungible tokens, and security token offerings.

NFT books provide a new application for NFTs, and they, like NFTs in the art and antique market, have several advantages. Customers' ownership rights are improved, writers are given new ways to promote their work, and new sorts of compelling material for potential customers are created. However, since NFT books are still in their infancy, the possibilities are limitless. The essential thing for creators to do right now is to study, explore, and find methods to get their works accessible on NFT markets (at fair pricing) and into the hands of readers in a straightforward manner.

This book is your one-stop store for getting a basic working grasp of the cryptocurrency markets and our financial suggestions. The crypto company's wall of technical smoke and mirrors must come crashing down, and this book represents a trained professional team rendering their hard-won knowledge as understandable as possible. To trade NFTs correctly, one doesn't need to become a math genius. You will, however, need a firm foundation of knowledge on which to grow. It's where you'll begin.

A special gift for you!

Thank you for reading this book.

If you enjoyed it, please visit the site where you purchased it and write a brief review. Your feedback is important to me and will help other readers decide whether to read the book too.

You are very important to me, so I decided to treat you with one of my bestsellers *"Option Trading Strategy"* or *"Blockchain 2021"*.
Please write me on nathanreal.books@gmail.com which of the 2 books you would like to receive for FREE.

Thank you!

—Nathan Real

Made in United States
North Haven, CT
09 March 2022

16972966R00068